"An innovative and hands-on guide that should be a must-read for everyone in business. It includes real life 'action steps' to more than effectively provide enthusiastic and energized customer service for today's modern and ever-changing client."

- Sheryl Daugherty, President, Arizona Tile Company

"Enjoyable and highly practical. Lis presents her extensive knowledge of customer service to readers and makes it fun by illustrating her points with her own experiences."

- Doug Ebersman, CPA

"This is an absolute must-read for all progressive thinking sales and customer service reps. Lis touches on the vitals of customer service. In her unique way, she articulates exactly how consumers want to be served today, what drives people into your stores, as well as what drives them away."

- John Wells, General Sales Manager, Taylor Flooring Ltd.

"After reading these '35 *sizzling ways to heat up your business and ignite your sales,*' you will be ready to join the ranks of those who succeed by holding on to their customers. You will also forever change how you approach the notion of customer service."

- Christine B. Whittemore, Chief Simplifier, Simple Marketing Now, LLC

"I've know Lisbeth for many years and she has successfully translated her passion in the classroom into print. As we enter this 'new era of customer service' it's refreshing to see that principles, values and loyalty still matter most."

- Mike Zoellner, VP Mohawk Marketing, Mohawk Industries

"Lis has highlighted one of the largest shortcomings in most businesses today. That is taking care of your old and present customers. After all, they have gotten you where you are and will take you where you are going."

- Kevin Gamble, Partner, 332 Flooring

RED HOT CUSTOMER SERVICE

35 SIZZLING WAYS TO HEAT UP YOUR BUSINESS AND IGNITE YOUR SALES

Lisbeth Calandrino

1st Edition

RED HOT CUSTOMER SERVICE

Lisbeth Calandrino

Copyright © 2009 by Lisbeth Calandrino
1st Edition
Printed in the United States of America

ISBN: 978-0-615-31185-2

Table of Contents

PART III: STAY ON TOP OF TRENDS

FOREWORD

About five years ago, a major national real estate firm asked consumers: "How important is great customer service?"

The answer, as you have guessed, is "extremely important." But here's the surprise: about 90% – 9 out of 10 – said quality service often determines if that company will get repeat business. Yes, getting the customer to come back again is a big, big deal.

And that's what Lis Calandrino's book *Red Hot Customer Service* is all about. Lis grew up learning about customer care from her father, a popular general contractor and remodeler. "He was successful in business. He was successful as a human being," Lis says. "He always made sure that everyone around him felt better having been a part of his life."

Lis, who's conducted training for many business owners, believes there's only one kind of customer service: the extraordinary kind. But how do you get there and build those habits into your daily routine?

Lis insists that your customers are your partners. Together, you can achieve great things. In this remarkable guide, she offers you all sorts of ideas for connecting with clients: by phone, by personal visits, by soliciting their advice... and more.

At the end of each chapter, she offers "action steps" to help you retain customers... and more important, to retain them as friends too.

Please enjoy – and learn – from this important, timely book.

- Rix Quinn

Rix Quinn is the author of Baby Boomers Speak!, *which chronicles the lives of people born between 1946-1964, and also* Words That Stick: A Guide to Short Writing with Big Impact.

To my dad, who knew the importance of treating every customer "as if they were the only customer." He proved that customer service could be translated into business profit.

ACKNOWLEDGEMENTS

I would like to acknowledge the following people for assisting me in the creation of this book. Chris Bowcutt for his expertise and insightful editorial skill. His good sense of humor made the process almost painless. To Nancy Reusswig who read and reread the manuscript, and Randy Rumph whose cover and cartoons added that special touch.

And of course to all of you who read the book as it was in process, gave me good ideas and were kind enough to support my efforts.

Thank you all very much.

Lis Calandrino

INTRODUCTION

Even as a child, business was part of my life. My father was a carpenter – or general contractor, or remodeler, depending on what era you come from – who owned his own business. I often accompanied him to job sites in those days. I risked skinned knees roller skating on concrete slabs that my father had poured (after the concrete cured, of course). I'd often eat with dad from his lunch box as we watched dad's employees – my uncles – work.

While my peers were off doing kids' stuff, I was unknowingly embarking on a business education. I watched how my father related to his customers, which seemed to be an art form. The work he did at customers' homes often carried over into phone calls to our house. While they usually came in the daytime, sometimes the customers would call in the evening. The time really didn't matter though, because customers were always welcome. You could even find these conversations taking place around our table on Sunday evenings as customers joined us for dinner. Meals were served with heaping portions, and there was no small amount of joking and laughter to go around.

Mom would sometimes get weary of the phone calls as they came in day and night, and I remember thinking *Hm, maybe she's right. Is this what you have to do to take care of customers? Isn't simply building their house enough*?

She tolerated it though, knowing well that dad was dad and that was just the way it was. In her own way I think she enjoyed having the folks around. So, they made the perfect "customer service pair." I still think that if the way to a *customer's* heart happens to be through his or her stomach, mom probably won dad many business projects.

No doubt, my father was successful. He was successful in business and he was successful as a human being. He always made sure that every one around him felt better having been a part of his life. He was, on a personal note, successful as a father as well. Was he rich? If quality of spirit is a measure of wealth, then he was rich. If wealth is measured by loyal and loving friends and customers, he was rich. If wealth is measured in customer satisfaction, dad was rich.

He recognized a lot of those intangibles and acted on them. That was the big reason for his success. Business is a human endeavor and he never lost focus on that. It did, in fact, earn him the expression, "Once Tony's customer, always Tony's customer!"

My dad's name was Tony.

Now I don't know if my business curiosity was genetic, learned, or a bit of both, but that curiosity blossomed at a young age. I remember dad peppering me with business-related questions. Sometimes, he'd also throw out a scenario for me to ponder, like, "One of my workers broke a lamp at Mrs. Wank's house. How should we handle it?"

Now that's a huge issue for a little girl not much taller than a coffee table to consider! Shouldn't I be out roller skating?

But the seed was planted. My interest in business and how it works began to grow. To this day, I'm still trying to satisfy that curiosity. In fact, for the last 20 years, I've traveled around the country conducting workshops and consulting, and listened to thousands of business owners express their thoughts on what works and what doesn't. As retailers, do you absolutely *have* to be big and rich? Do you absolutely *have* to be well-financed or have celebrities shopping in your store to satisfy customers and make money?

I've concluded there's more to it than that. It seems that the secret is something people are calling *exclamatory customer service*, or – a new buzz word I've heard lately – *bonding* with your customers. Not hard to do, but in order to do it one has to not only step out of the box, but realize that the box never existed. Companies that flourish take risks; and not necessarily monetary risks, but risks of thought and idea. It seems that people are more willing to take monetary risks if it's worked before or if their competitor is doing it. The real growth and success is in the unknown and the willingness to go the extra mile.

And there are people who are willing to do it. They just do things that others won't do. It's what businesses refer to as the "added value." It's providing exceptional customer service and treating customers like they want to be treated. So, as this all relates to this book, I thought it might be useful as well as fun to look at what works, what doesn't, and what you can do differently.

In September of 2007, the Dallas-based luxury department store chain Neiman Marcus celebrated its 100th birthday. The company, noted for its signature chocolate chip cookies, gave away not only cookies but the actual recipe in celebration of their centennial event. Weren't they afraid their competitors or customers would simply duplicate the product? Whether they did or didn't, it doesn't seem to be affecting their bottom line. Their ranking in the Fortune 1000 hardly changed over the course of the year (ranked #517 in 2007 and #513 in 2008).

Cookies may not be the biggest deal in the grand scheme of things, but it can be if it's the central component of your business and livelihood. For Neiman Marcus, clearly it's not the central component. It's not the same as Coke giving away its famous recipe. But I still find what they did fascinating. They took a risk and gave something away for free. And it looks like it's helped them more than anything.

So, dear reader, think of this as a cookbook. This book contains recipes for good business. It's been many years in the baking! And it started in my father's kitchen.

PART I

WHAT'S OLD IS NEW

Chapter 1

TAKE CARE OF THE CUSTOMER

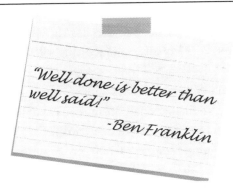

"Well done is better than well said!"

-Ben Franklin

You're probably wondering: why read another book on customer service? What could possibly be new or how has it changed? Well, it's not so much a matter of whether it's old or new, it's a matter of whether you're taking the following message in:

Take care of the customer!

I came across an interesting statistic about Fortune 500 companies recently. As of 1979, 70% of the companies that had dominated the 20th century were out of business. As of 2000, another 30% were gone. Considering how easily a (one-time) Fortune 500 can go under, one can only ask, "What's the little guy to do?" Especially when the economy is shattered?

Take heart, because it's actually the little guys that form the basis of our economy – no matter what state it's in. According to the Small Business Association, as of 2004, small businesses (100 employees or less):

- Represent more than 99.7% of all employers
- Employ half of all private-sector workers and 39% of workers in high-tech jobs

- Provide 60% to 80% of the net new jobs annually
- Pay 44.3% of total U.S. private payroll
- Produce more than 50% of non-farm private gross domestic product, or a GDP of roughly $6 trillion
- Are 3% franchises
- Account for 52.6% of all retail sales, 46.8% of all wholesale sales, and 24.8% of all manufacturing sales

Clearly, small businesses pack a lot of punch when it comes to our economy. But what makes small businesses capable of competing with – or even out-competing – the big companies? According to successful small business owners, amongst whom I consider my father, the key is being able to *hold on to your customers.*

There are different approaches to doing this, most of which are very basic. Some, however, require just a little twist. For example:

- **Change the language**. Take the word "customers" and turn it into "investors." Thinking of them as investors means they should be getting a long-term reward for their purchase – something that continually grows and brings rewards.
- Make sure your employees know that **nothing is more important than the investor** (i.e. the customer) – and give them the tools to ensure that's what they're promoting.
- **Always be improving**. These are small changes that your business makes slowly over time. At first, these changes may not be readily apparent, but over time they will be noticeable.
- **Don't let "old customers" slip away**. Most companies slowly add new customers to the top of the pile while old customers slowly slip away. Let's say that one company has a retention rate of 95% and another has 90%. One company loses 5% a year and the other 10%. If each company acquires new customers at 10% per year, the first will have a 5% net

growth in customer inventory per year while the other will have none. If you look at this over a number of years, the results are staggering.

- Spend as much time tracking customer inventory as you do product inventory. **The best inventory you have is your customer**. Remember, it costs six times as much to bring in a new customer as it does to keep an old customer.

- **Figure out** *why* **your customers buy the products they do** from you. You might think you know, but do you really? Once you're more sure, you can start tailoring your sales and marketing strategy accordingly.

- Find unique ways to make customers a priority and go out of your way to keep them.

Remember, when it comes to customer service, what's tried is true, what's old is new.

Action steps

- Take inventory of your customers.
- What strategies have you developed for replacing lost customers?
- In what ways do you currently work to make customers a priority?

Date for review:

Chapter 2

THE CUSTOMER IS THE KEY TO YOUR BUSINESS

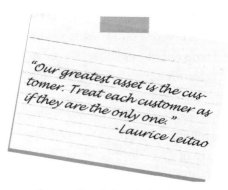

"Our greatest asset is the customer. Treat each customer as if they are the only one."

-Laurice Leitao

Over the years I've realized that it isn't just one thing that holds companies together; it's a multitude of things. Service will always revolve around the customer. At a glance, this seems easy; all you have to do is treat them right, right? The question is, what is right and how do you know it's right?

In business, one size does not fit all. How can that be, you say? Most people are alike and we all simply want to be treated well. However, treat your customers all the same and there's one thing I can guarantee you: they won't be customers for long!

My father said, "Everyone's different—and they like it that way." In other words, don't make your customers all alike. Strive to keep them different, to know what each one likes. Tony used to make up pet names for his customers. The Sattenspiels were known as the "garbage pails." Offensive, you say? Maybe. But the customers loved it knowing that Tony had spent time coming up with these little nick names! Plus, they knew him and knew his intentions were always good.

What You Build

The movie *Field of Dreams* memorialized the saying, "Build it and they will come." Well, that was nothing more than a line in a movie. Just because you build a store doesn't mean the customer-equivalent of Shoeless Joe Jackson is going to show up. We're already over-built with retail space and consumers have more choices than they need or want. Oh, and even if he does show up, it still doesn't matter unless he *buys* something. That's the bottom line.

While the customer is king these days, in the old days it didn't matter how you treated them. The only thing that was alike back then was the merchandise and how it was sold. You could treat customers the same – or even with indifference – and still make money because there was a shortage of merchandise. If you wanted it, you had to buy what was offered and how it was offered, because that's all that was offered! In fact, it was the *customers* who were afraid to mistreat business owners, because there were so few places to shop. I can remember my mom once chiding me in a store, saying, "Lissy, behave, if Mr. Charles throws us out there'll be no place in town to shop for shoes."

Fast forward to today. What a difference! Customers can do whatever they want in the store without worrying about getting thrown out. In fact, if they do get thrown out they'll probably turn around and sue the proprietor.

A funny fact about what customers were willing to put themselves through back in the "olden days." When television sets first came out in the late 1930s, tens of thousands of people bought them even though it was difficult to get a good picture. Only those who lived up on hills could get good reception. It wasn't until the 1950s that Marvin Middlemark patented the "rabbit ears" T.V. antenna, making good reception a mainstream reality. It still makes me laugh to think that customers, including my family, were willing to purchase T.V. sets that really didn't show a decent picture. Goes to show how powerful trends can be.

But of course, that was in the infancy stage of retailing, before the Internet, before blogs, before social networking applications, before mass-produced computers and certainly before Angie's List. Products weren't so quickly subjected to customer review. All people knew was they had to have the product, even if it didn't function as hoped!

CUSTOMERS NOW KNOW MORE

Back then, customers didn't know what they didn't know, and the store owners had the upper hand – they had the knowledge. Customers were pretty much treated as if they were to be tolerated, and if they wanted to return something, they'd better have that invoice and do it within thirty days.

Retailer was king!

My friend once went to Home Depot to return plumbing fixtures. Not only were the fixtures 10 years old, but she hadn't even purchased them from Home Depot! The store still wrote her a credit. Can you believe it? In the old days, the first thing the store would have asked was, "Do you have a receipt?"

As a result of the Internet, customers know what they know as well as what they don't know – and often it's more than the salesperson knows. As a store owner, you may have found yourself competing with some Internet guru's words that your customers have latched onto. There's something to be said about that – customers have the tools to be more informed than ever. It doesn't mean that the Web is always right, but there's a lot more information available now.

So remember, not all customers are alike and you really can't treat them all the same. The Golden Rule isn't always in play. I laugh when people say, "I wouldn't like it if the customer treated me that way." How you or I want to be treated is not at issue. It's the customer's standards that are important. The higher their standards, the better it is for us to ensure we're providing quality goods and services.

So, what can you do?

- **Treat customers the way they want to be treated**. That's the way it is. Those who get it will win, those who don't will fall down the rabbit hole. In the book, *Who Moved my Cheese?* we found that those willing to adapt were able to succeed. When the cheese was moved the mice knew enough to look elsewhere. They were willing to change. Are you?
- **Realize that the good old days were just that: good, and old**. Or maybe just old and not even that good. It doesn't really matter, because those days won't be back. As my mother Marie used to say about fashion: what goes around comes around but it never looks quite the same, so don't save your old clothes. In those days they hadn't yet heard about "vintage" – old was simply old. When I asked mom if the doctor who delivered me was good, she said, "Who knows? He was willing to make house calls and he had good manners!"
- **Consider reinventing yourself**. Remember, insanity is defined as doing the same things over and over again and expecting different results. How will you know who to be and what to do? Your customers will know. Look at Madonna. She's a regular "quick change" artist and it works!
- **The customer comes in for a new experience**, not just to purchase a product. They're all different and they want different things – just like the people in your life whom you're trying to please on a daily basis. Once you get that figured out in life you've got it knocked and life is good. The same with your customers.
- **Customers become difficult only when they aren't getting what they want**. So you'll have to decide: can I give them what they want or not? Customers don't mind paying for an experience. You just have to provide it.

Bottom line: give customers what they want.

Action steps

- Compose a list of what you believe your customers expect.
- List specific experiences that you provide that meet these expectations.
- What new experiences could you develop for your customers?

Date for review:

Chapter 3

HEAT UP YOUR SALESPEOPLE – LOYALTY STARTS FROM WITHIN

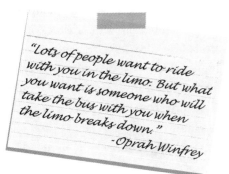

"Lots of people want to ride with you in the limo. But what take the bus with you will the limo breaks down."

-Oprah Winfrey

If employees don't understand what customer loyalty means to the business, they will not manage to create enough value to cover even their salaries. Employees must constantly be building partnerships with their customers and constantly be thinking about how to instill loyalty in them.

To create customer loyalty, we must first build *employee* loyalty. This means hiring the right people – those who've developed a sense of ethics and personal values – and then helping them see how (or if) your company's values are similar to their own. Very few people can simply "do their own thing" in any given business and see it contribute to office unity. Rather, there needs to be commonality in goals and values for a company to truly make it. It's common knowledge that franchise start-ups have a survival rate of two- to three-times that of independent start-ups. The difference is that franchises already have clear systems, clear benchmarks and a clear vision in place. They have track records.

Customers are not loyal to new products, or to a better showroom or to cheaper prices. Customers build loyalty to those who deliver the service they're looking for. You may be selling products, but the *way* those products are sold and delivered is the service.

Loyalty is a fine line between the salesperson's self-interest and the customer's interests. Funny how employers sometimes talk about sales commission as if it were evil; I've heard that commissions can cause salespeople to steal sales and not assist customers who "don't belong to them." Make sure your salespeople can earn a decent living first, and the commission becomes the frosting on the cake.

As you probably already know, closing rates of referred customers are higher than those not referred. Why? Because referred customers have a tendency to be already loyal by the time they get to your business. Court those referred customers – go out of your way for them and let them know they're special.

Also, who in your place knows how to deliver the goods? Identify profitable employees and pay close attention to them: What do they do that makes them memorable? Is it a comforting statement or a nice gesture? Do they carry samples to the customer's car? Do they send thank you notes to everyone for coming into your store?

When I was in the furniture business I had a salesman who used to promise his customers he would marry them if they bought a product. This worked for about a month until it came back to haunt him. Who knew some customers might want him to make good on the offer?

One of the stores I currently consult with has a salesman who tells all the customers he loves them. Yes, he loves them. The store has never been sued and the salesman has never been up on charges. There's something about the way he says it that makes you want to love him back. He's not even remotely good looking – maybe that's why he can get away with what he says. Why does it mean so much to his customers? "Because it's real," he says.

THE POWER OF TOUCH

Americans are not the most touchy-feely sort. We may be outgoing, boisterous, friendly, caring and quite often loving, but we're not exactly touchy-feely. At least in public. There is, however, something to be said about the power of touch.

I read an interesting study recently about the power of touch – and by that I mean the actual physical act of touching someone. In an experiment, a researcher asked a couple of strangers at a beach to watch his bicycle while he went to the snack bar. While he was gone, the bike was stolen. Interestingly, not one of the strangers tried to stop the thief.

In the second scenario, the researcher not only asked the strangers to watch the bike, but touched one of them on the arm in the process. The same result happened: the bike was stolen. However, in this case the strangers yelled or ran after the thief. Additional experiments showed that 90% of the time, strangers yelled or ran after the thief after having been touched in the initial interaction.

Now, I'm not suggesting you advise employees to go and smother the next customer who walks in the door. Touch – like any technique used to gain rapport – is learned. What this teaches is that an act as simple as a touch can be used to create an instant connection.

Pay close attention to what your staff is doing to get results. Is it a smile, a touch on the customer's arm or a comforting statement? Do they go the extra mile to help out? When you've discovered the ones who stand out, take care of them. Reward them, pay them for what they produce rather than what they do to keep busy. Pay everyone for results that impact the bottom line. Determine the "net worth" of each employee. If the bottom line is to *impact* the bottom line, figure out what it is and reward people for behaviors that go directly to what makes a difference.

On the other hand, if you find an employee's performance has deteriorated, send him to a class, a training or somewhere where he can get motivated to get back on track. We all get worn out from time to time. Also, it will keep them on their toes knowing that you mean business.

KEEPING YOUR INTERNAL CUSTOMERS HAPPY

It bears repeating: we are all customers. If you're an employee in a business, you're the internal customer. Your attitude, moreover, will dictate much of your performance. If you're happy about your place of employment and love the products, you are more likely to attract customers. If you openly talk about how unfair your boss is to you and how awful the products are, you will have trouble selling.

I remember talking with employees at the Container Store after the store had just been voted one of the best places to work. I asked several of them if the store really *was* that great. I mean, what can be so great about selling containers? Much to my surprise, every one of them commented on how well they were treated by management. They were clear about the company's path and felt they had a good future. Certainly not what I hear a lot of times in training at other stores.

It's easy to see how a happy employee influences customers and sells more. But what keeps that employee – the internal customer – happy?

It's not just pay. Employers who pay good salaries will say that's what makes employees productive. I know several places that pay well but feature unhappy employees. Earning a good salary is certainly part of the mix, but so is being treated fairly, feeling that you're on a winning team and feeling purposeful in what you do.

How about your attitude as an employee? If your attitude is positive, you will be able to get over small problems and do the right thing. If you find fault with everything in life, then work is just another place for you to complain. Remember the old expression: If you're not part of the solution, you're probably part of the problem.

If you're an employer, you may have heard that the number one reason employees leave is because of unclear expectations. Employees want to know if they have a future in the business – and what that future requires of them.

Ask your employees what would make them happy. Does this seem like a scary question? Someone might say, "A million dollars," and you now know you'll never be able to please them. You'll more likely hear someone say, "I'd love an afternoon off so I can go see my kid's soccer game," or, "I'd love to work from home one day a week."

It's the little things that add to the satisfaction of our everyday lives.

KICK YOUR EMPLOYEES UP A NOTCH

There's a book by Sam Parker called *212: The Extra Degree* that I recommend picking up. It talks about how water is scalding at 211 degrees F (or 99.5 degrees Celsius). However, at 212 degrees F (100 degrees Celsius) it boils – *surprise!* – and turns into steam.

In other words, while hot water can boil an egg, steam can power a train! And the difference is a matter of only one degree.

The concept is simple but still significant. What magnificent changes could I make if I just kicked things up another notch?

Just working 15 minutes a day is what helped me finish this book. Did it take long? Who cares? It got done. I just had to "heat myself up" a notch. What if I went and turned it up to an even greater degree?

The key for you is to figure out what one degree more from your employees will create, and then help them access it.

Sometimes it doesn't take very much. Here's an anecdote from *212* that illustrates the difference in one degree of effort.

> From 2000-2006, The PGA Championship winner took home
> an average of $1,060,714. The second place finisher averaged
> $460,657 less. The margin of difference: 1.171 strokes.

Just one stroke resulted in a difference of $600K in earnings. It reminds me of the struggle many people face with respect to losing weight. I once counseled a woman who was 200 pounds overweight.

Try as she might, she said she just couldn't do it. She was always on the road, she said – always in her car and addicted to cookies. Girl Scout cookies, specifically. I asked her how many cookies she ate a day and she said she didn't know. I asked if she wouldn't mind just filling a box with cookies and eating as many as she wanted for the week and then reporting back. As it turned out, she ate about 100 a week! I then asked if she would try a little experiment. I asked her to take 200 cookies with her for a week, and promise to eat them all. She couldn't believe it. You probably know how it went. By the next week she thought she was going to die from cookie consumption. So I suggested she eat five fewer cookies a day.

In about a month she was down to five cookies a day and the pounds were rolling off. She began to enjoy the "not full feeling." We eventually got her down to one cookie a day.

This helps to illustrate how small goals are necessary in order to achieve the larger goals. A powerful motivator for your employees is to get them to work together as a team, to share their goals and to want to help each other attain those goals.

There are several things you can introduce to your business to help heat things up. Give your staff products to wear, test drive or install in their homes. Make it the good stuff – stuff they normally couldn't buy for themselves. Give them a "one notch" experience to brag about – an experience they can share with their customers.

If you walk into Victoria's Secret, you'll find the salespeople ready to find you exactly what you're looking for. This is because they're given products to take home, and therefore can talk to you about it based on their own experience.

Think about how many times you've gone into a restaurant and asked the server how the lobster was, only to hear, "I don't know, I can't afford it!" Not the most helpful way for a restaurant to sell the big ticket items.

Help your salespeople know what they're selling.

Another way to kick things up a notch in your workplace: Change the way your employees look. Encourage them to be classy, professional and business-like in their attire. Only if you own a Hooters store should your employees look like they work at Hooters. Develop a code for "good looks." You don't want your employees looking like they work at an auto shop – with matching shirts with name tags. That attire has its place, and it's not in your business. Help your employees understand that caring about what they wear is caring not only about the customer, but about their own success.

You're not asking them to change their belief system. You're simply asking them to not come to work in ripped jeans and belly shirts!

Teach your employees to be respectful of their customers and your store, and most importantly of themselves. Always aim for the best and to constantly strive to be better. You're aiming for that one extra degree, remember – that temperature where everything changes.

GOOD TEAMS WILL WIN ALL THE TIME

I remember when there was an ongoing debate among the L.A. Lakers about whether they could pull off a winning season without Kobe Bryant. Bryant has, after all, paved the way for much of the team's success in recent years. At the same time, Bryant wouldn't be who he is without the team to support him.

When you look at your staff, do you see a team of players working in support of a superstar; or are there superstars working for themselves? Truth be told, none of these approaches is bad at all. If the setting is harmonious and everyone's getting the job done, why not keep it? If, however, there's acrimony and some employees insist on doing things that are counterproductive to the business, you need to put your foot down. After all, the purpose of a team is to work together to fulfill the team's goals, *which should include the individual's goals.*

I'll go into stores sometimes and notice the "renegade" salesperson – the one who doesn't have to do his paperwork, who makes his own work schedule and basically can't be counted on to do anything other than what he wants to do! He might even be a top producer. Often times the owner is afraid to ask this person to join in or be part of the team for fear that the person will leave if he doesn't get his own way. Typically when this person leaves – and they often do – all kinds of improprieties are discovered. In any major league team the renegades are only tolerated for a short time. Why? Because they destroy morale and take away from the growth of others.

So how do you run the team? There are many different styles of management, but gone is the "beat 'em up and leave the dead ones in the road" mentality. I'll use an illustration from a (truly) classic T.V. show, *Leave it to Beaver.*

The show revolves around the antics of a boy named Theodore, who's otherwise known as the Beaver. The Beaver is young and full of pranks. But whenever "the Beav" goes astray, his father Ward takes it upon himself to set the boy straight. The scenarios tend to go something like this:

> Ward learns that the Beav has been up to mischief again. He glares at him with a stern face. "What do you have to say for yourself, young man?"

> The Beaver fidgets in his dad's presence, typically making up excuses for his behavior. He's clearly intimidated.

> Ward continues to interrogate him and to show him who's boss.

> June, the mother, takes her husband aside and gives him some friendly advice. "When you talk to Theodore why not let him know you're on his side?"

> Ward softens and expresses more compassion for his son.

All is well.

Ward, as you can see, represents old time leadership – the traditional authority figure: *Tell them who's boss and then teach them how to act.*

June is more like the group leader, or the good cop. She tries to inspire everyone to work together. She doesn't judge anyone, she just knows in the long run if they all work together through cooperation and common goals, it will work out better in the end. She will also accomplish what she needs to get done with little effort and less stress.

Team work wins out. But working as a team isn't always easy. Some members want to win and want all the glory; they don't care about the team or the goal as long as they look good.

Working as a team means there needs to be trust and an understanding of the challenges that everyone faces.

As an owner or manager, one needs to be in tune with these challenges while at the same time empathetic to people's emotions and limitations.

Building togetherness is important, and it takes time – time possibly away from your business. How about a day when everyone can go somewhere that is not work related to engage in some team-building exercises? You can try white water rafting, low ropes, or any activity where people need to depend on one another to succeed.

You can, once every couple of months, host an employee dinner and treat your staff to an outing.

Some other ideas:

- Help your employees develop interpersonal skills; give them positive feedback so that they'll feel motivated to improve. Give them goals so they can live up to high standards.
- Let the team know how important they are to the overall success of the mission.

- Be positive, treat your employees the way you want them to treat your customers.

EMPLOYEE RETENTION

In a study conducted by Robert Half International, 1000 executives at some of the nation's largest companies were asked: "Which of the following is most likely to cause good employees to quit their jobs?"

Their responses were:

- Limited opportunities for advancement: 39%
- Unhappiness with management: 23%
- Lack of recognition: 17%
- Inadequate salary and benefits: 11%
- Bored with their job: 6%
- Lifestyle change (moving, etc.): 2%
- Other/don't know: 2%

As an employer (or future employer), there are things that you can do early on to deal with the above issues and help retain your good employees.

Issue: Limited opportunities for advancement

Learn what your employees' goals are and ensure that their jobs help to fulfill them. Be a good coach. Learn to *coach* your employees to success rather than manage them. Your business should be a place for growth among the staff. Even if there's limited room for advancement – and there are plenty of businesses where this is simply the case – there is never a limit on how much one can grow within himself while on the job. It's up to you to constantly be providing new ways for your staff to grow and improve themselves.

Issue: Unhappiness with management

Be clear in your message and what your principles are. Spend time with employees to build understanding between one another. There's a difference between unhappiness with one's job and unhappiness with one's employers.

Issue: Lack of recognition

Show employees that you trust and value them. When they do a good job, tell them; if it's not so good don't berate them. Simply help them get back on track. A mistake, whether major or minor, is not the end of the world, and shouldn't be the end of one's job.

Issue: Inadequate salary and benefits

Find ways for your employees to make money. They don't simply have to be on salary. Anyone who works for you can bring in customers and therefore be eligible for a commission. How about the guy in the warehouse? Can he bring in a customer? Can your bookkeeper bring in a customer? Customers mean money.

Issue: Bored with their job

I consider boredom to be a choice. Anyone can create challenges for themselves to spice things up – so why not help them? How about contests or friendly competitions among employees? You can add a charitable component to your goals and provide a way for employees to feel like they're contributing to the community.

Issue: Lifestyle change

Plenty of people simply relocate or move into other industries. Do what you can to support them.

Issue: Other/don't know

Well, if you don't know the problem, can you prescribe a solution?

Creating a strong team and helping to retain your good employees requires defining goals and rewarding those who excel. Hire for attitude and not just knowledge. Knowledge can be taught; attitude is tough to teach and it's hard to get rid of bad ones.

Action steps

- What type of employee incentives do you have in place?
- What have you added to "brighten up" this program?
- Are you currently collecting feedback from your staff on how to improve the work environment?
- List 3-5 new things you can add.

Date for review:

Chapter 4

THINK OF CUSTOMERS AS PARTNERS

Partner - n. One that is united or associated with another or others in an activity or a sphere of common interest.

Build a partnership with your customers. "Customer service" sometimes sounds like something you do *for* the customer. A partnership, on the other hand, implies *equal* – something you do for each other.

You probably remember the news clip a few years ago where a man sued his dry cleaners for an exorbitant amount of money because they lost a pair of his pants. When they tried to settle with him for what seemed like a more than fair amount, he upped the ante to a few million dollars. He lost in court, but not before the dry cleaners wished they'd never heard his name.

This clearly was not a business transaction between those with a "partner" mentality. While one side certainly made a mistake, they at least offered to make things right. The other side simply was in search of a big payday.

The lesson in this is sometimes there will be unreasonable customers and you'll have to deal with them. But for every sue-happy customer, there will be scores of reasonable ones – those who are more than happy to form a partnership with you. To minimize incidences when it comes to your business, simply find out what works and keep doing it.

How will you know if it works? For one, you'll start getting the results you've been looking for. It reminds me of the old joke where someone asks, "Why are you beating your head against the wall?" "Because it feels better when I stop," the other person says.

The only way you'll know if it gets better is if you stop doing what is hurting you right now.

Act like your customers are your partners and that you value them – even if you have to give them cute nick names to keep your sanity, like Tony.

Action Steps

- Name 10 customers who you consider to be partners; how are you supporting these partnerships?
- What can you do to convert other customers into partners?

Date for review:

Chapter 5

LET CUSTOMERS TELL YOU HOW THEY WANT TO BE TREATED

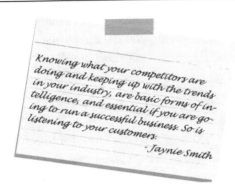

Knowing what your competitors are doing and keeping up with the trends in your industry, are basic forms of intelligence, and essential if you are going to run a successful business. So is listening to your customers.

- Jaynie Smith

According to statistics compiled by the White House Office of Customer Affairs, Technical Assistance Research Programs (TARP):

- 96% of unhappy customers never complain
- 91% of those who do not complain will not buy again from the business that offended them
- The average unhappy customer will share their negative story with at least 9 other people
- 13% will tell more than 20 people
- The average unhappy customer will talk about the unpleasant experience for 18 months.

What do you think this means?

It means you have to do everything in your power to ensure your customers have a positive experience in your business. You may not be able to read their minds, but you can always ask them how they like your product or service. It never hurts to ask!

Here are several angles you can adopt to help elicit information about how you're doing.

- **Hire someone to stand outside your store and survey customers**. Why can't you do it yourself? Because you won't be as objective. You'll spend your time apologizing for something you did. Plus, your customers might feel uncomfortable giving you the direct feedback.

- **Make sure the questions you ask make sense.** I came out of the doctor's office once and was asked if I would complete a survey for $1 (which was certainly a twist on the old "a penny for your thoughts" routine!). The questions they asked, however, weren't the most direct or relevant (e.g. "How did your visit go?" "Do you feel you'll get better as a result of coming in today?"). The key is to ask questions designed to elicit the most specific, measurable information possible. Have them quantify the experience as much as possible. It's similar to speaking to a child. If you ask a yes/no question, you get a yes/no answer and the conversation is over. Instead, focus on asking open-ended questions that will help the child (or customer) think more deeply and express more fully (e.g. "What's the longest you would be willing to wait in the waiting room prior to seeing your doctor?" "What could we change to help you be more comfortable next time?").

- **Conduct phone surveys**. To add levity to the situation, you can even have your mom (or a relative) call. "My son just fixed your roof; did he do a good job? Let me know because I'll give him hell at Sunday dinner if he didn't!"

- **Leave surveys at the customer's house**. If you're in a business where going to the customer's house is customary, leave a survey with a self-addressed stamped envelope.

- **Quantify your questions**. Create a rating system from one to 10. Once you get yourself rated you can publish the results on your Web site or send it to the newspaper. Why get numbers? Because numbers are proof. "95% of our customers say the cherry pie is worth eating," or "95% of our customers survived the cherry pie."

- **Inform your employees**. Once you have customer feedback, share it with your employees. Don't give out the customer's name – it might come back to haunt you if you advertised an anonymous survey.

- **Listen to the feedback**. You may get some new ideas or you may even be told to scrap your idea. In any event, listen to the customers. Maybe you won't like what you hear. That doesn't matter. What matters is that what they say makes a difference to the customer. Remember: Customers are the ones that count.

- **Work the bugs out of it until you know what works**. Hey, if enough customers think your store hours are inconvenient, why wouldn't you want to change them?

- **Give customers what they want**. You'll know if it's really good if your competitors copy it. After they copy it, get better and change it.

- **Keep motivated**. Complacency will kill everything. Keep changing and making things better. Just because things are good doesn't mean they can't be better. Nobody ever went out of business because they were too good to customers. Unless, of course, they thought that dropping all their prices was being good.

- **Ask for a referral**. After the job is done, call your customers and ask what they think. If the customer says "great!" then ask for a referral. If there's a problem, fix it.

- **Listen**. Ask your customers questions and then *listen* to what they want and need.

- **Write it down**. In this era of technology, it is imperative to have a computerized system to manage and control customer information. Software such as ACT or even something as basic as Microsoft Excel will help you keep tabs on customer information and where they are in the sales process.

Action steps

- What do you need to know about your policies?
- Develop a customer feedback survey and hire someone to collect the data.
- Determine how you will use the information.

Date for review:

Chapter 6

RAPPORT IS KEY TO COMMUNICATION

Think about it. if you made one new friend or business acquaintance a month, you would have 12 more for the year. If you kept in touch and built exponentially, who knows how many you would have?

Smile! As simple as it sounds, it makes a world of difference.

Also, as cliché as it sounds, your attitude *does* define much of how successful you will be.

What type of attitude do you project?

What you think and feel is typically what you project – and what you project comes to be known as your attitude. If you're happy, people know it; if you're not, they know that too.

It's in the tone of your voice and the look on your face. Have you ever been around someone who's convinced they're not angry, and to drive the point home they yell "I'm not angry!" at you?

Do you come across as warm and friendly or as unapproachable? What do you think about people you don't know? Do you think they're friendly or unfriendly? How you think about these things describes much about you.

There are behaviors you can use to help gain rapport in any situation. Consider these:

- When you speak to people, face your whole body to them, "belly button to belly button." When you have your side to them that's what's known as the cold shoulder and it indicates to people that you'd rather be elsewhere.

- Stand still. Don't fidget when you're talking to people. Listen to how people talk; listen to their tone and their speech rate and match it.
- Project an open and upbeat attitude. Let them know you are there to help, and you know what you're talking about.
- Don't cross your arms while speaking to customers. This may sound ridiculous, but by crossing your arms you are inadvertently closing them off. Don't cross your arms in front of you even if you need to keep warm.
- Synchronize with them! Customers who see that they're speaking with someone similar to them will feel more comfortable talking, and in turn feel better about buying something.
- Always offer your first name when introducing yourself.
- Make eye contact and keep eye contact. When you rise out of the chair, stand up straight so you can maintain eye contact. Leaning forward is how we usually do it, but it often makes us break eye contact. This takes some practice but you will feel the difference.
- Ask them open-ended questions, which will allow them to do more talking and in turn help you collect more information.
- Actively listen and lean forward. Body language is everything – more is said with your body than with words.
- Write down what your customer says when it's appropriate.
- Compliment or praise people for things that matter. Find something you like and tell them you like it.
- Look for the good and unusual – not the ordinary.
- Acknowledge somebody's presence. Never let someone walk through the door without being properly greeted.
- No one wants to be fake, so don't be! Make a meaningful statement, even if it's something as simple as, "I love those shoes!"

- Appreciate people for who they are and what they have to offer. Everyone has something to offer. "Wow, you have quite a task in front of you but you seem up for the challenge." Looking for the good stuff will keep your attitude positive.
- Be attentive. If, in the midst of a conversation, a customer mentions a particular situation that's similar to yours, comment on it. This is how you will connect. Customers will be surprised you were paying that much attention, and thankful that you actually took the time for them.
- Slow down. In today's fast-paced world it seems that no one has time for anyone or anything. If you take the time to have a real conversation with a customer, he'll feel that you've put a special interest in him, and will feel appreciated. A customer who feels appreciated is much more likely to buy from you than one who feels like he's been brushed off.

On a flight from San Antonio some years ago, I sat next to a woman named Linda who was on her way north to help her daughter through a divorce. Not a vacation for her, obviously. Her daughter had a young child and not much money. Linda explained that she had left her nursing job in order to take care of her daughter. Well, when we landed, there was so much snow that her daughter couldn't pick her up. I invited Linda to stay with me—which she did for three days. When the roads were safer, I drove her to her daughter's. She vowed to help me if ever I needed it. Two years later I came down with cancer and I called Linda. Over the next year and a half she helped me through my ordeal. We've been friends ever since.

Action steps

- Develop a series of internal workshops on rapport building.

Date for review:

Chapter 7

PUT FIRE IN YOUR COMMUNICATION – IT'S THE KEY TO SUCCESS

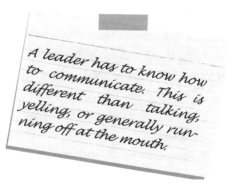

A leader has to know how to communicate. This is different than talking, yelling, or generally running off at the mouth.

Speak slowly! If you're a New Yorker, like I am, this goes double for you. People want to hear and understand what you're saying without having to ask "*What?*" over and over again.

A friend of mine in New Orleans fell in love with a Yankee girl who manned an order desk at one of his supplier's stores. He liked the up-front, direct talk she used. He used to close his eyes and wonder what she looked like. He finally met her – and was disappointed. Maybe he should have kept the relationship strictly phone-based!

Customers' needs are always changing, whether it's in fashion, technology or their reactions to the economy. By watching changes in the economy you will begin to understand change in society. Changes in society affect all businesses. Remember, you can't run your business in a bubble or the bubble of your mind. Long-term profitability is tied to customers, and customers will only buy what they want.

So keep up with changing needs and look for ways to capitalize on them. Remember when Heinz came out with blue and green ketchup? Most adults were appalled by the color and weren't interested. It didn't really matter though – if you were over 10 years old you probably weren't the target customer. I bought the green ketchup just so I could be involved!

Sounds obvious, but bad breath is one way to prevent good in-person communication. Invest in breath mints. Coffee, onions, garlic and Italian dressing have no place in retail. No matter how much you like garlic, someone is bound to be offended.

Like your Mother taught you, always say "please" and "thank you" and "excuse me." I can't believe how many people sneeze and belch without covering their mouths and noses. I've also noticed that a lot of the offenders aren't necessarily from the U.S., though we certainly do have our own share of ill-mannered citizens. This brings to mind a documentary I saw covering one of McDonald's massive openings in a foreign market. The company said the hardest part of the process was simply getting the employees to wash their hands! My friend who just returned from this country's capital had more to say on the subject, but I think you get the point.

Make sure your employees feel comfortable enough with you to go to you if they feel there is a problem in the store. Being the boss means you have to be accessible.

Answer customers' questions quickly and take their concerns as important. Ask yourself, how would someone feel after dealing with you? Are you sure that they will feel positive and that you've left them with a good impression?

I sometimes hear salespeople say, "I'm not going to put up with that," when there's a troublesome customer. Remember the expression about turning lemons into lemonade? If you want to keep your customers, make the most of any situation – especially customer complaints.

If you have a problem with a customer, remember that you don't have to like her – you just have to get her what she wants. Open up your lines of communication and make sure you ask enough questions so your customer can share her expectations with you.

GET TO THE HEART OF THE MATTER

Don't show your product too soon, no matter how eager the customer is or how little patience you have. Spending time assessing needs as well as the customer's expectations will go a long way. You can't help anyone make a decision until you understand him.

When I bought my first computer years ago, the first question the salesman asked was, "How fast do you want it to go?" I had absolutely no idea what he meant. He kept repeating the same question until I asked him, "Can you put it another way?" He then came up with an analogy. He said some computers are like a Jaguar, and others are like a Ford Focus. I got it then. Having owned both cars, I was sure I wanted a Jaguar.

Ask your customers questions they understand and give only enough information to help them make a decision. Anything more will just confuse them.

Do you and your customers prefer staying on track? Lapsing off into what you did over the weekend doesn't add to the decision-making process for most people. For example, if you call your insurance company, chances are they'll ask you to have your policy number ready. This is a shared expectation. You now know what they need of you for them to be able to help you get what you need from them. Unless your customers buy your product often, they don't know what to bring or what to expect.

Ask questions that are non-threatening and that will get the person to feel comfortable and talk. Remember Colombo? Or more recently, Monk? What makes these characters so endearing are the questions they ask their "persons of interest." They start with normal questions such as "Where were you on Friday?" or "What did you have for lunch?" before throwing in a random question like, "Where can I get a good cigar?" The aim is to change the suspects' train of thought, get them off the subject and then see if they can get them to relax so they'll spill the beans!

Try to clue into whether your customers have time to chat or just want to get to the point!

Like a good investigator, you're on a subtle fact-finding mission when interacting with the customer. Someone who's in a rush doesn't want to feel stuck because you keep talking, while on the other hand, someone who wants this attention doesn't want to feel brushed off and pushed out the door. Follow their lead, let them set the pace. Try and put yourself in their shoes. By doing this, you'll better be able to tell them what they need to know, in a way they'll understand.

Be enthusiastic. Nothing goes further in enrolling a customer in you than a happy attitude. The same goes for the person who looks for solutions rather than problems and thinks "win-win" for everyone rather than "win-lose."

Customers love to see that you're excited about what you're selling. Why? Because what you're selling is what they want to buy. If you believe in it, why shouldn't they? Your believing in what you're doing makes others more comfortable about what they're buying.

I went into a shoe store once looking for a very simple and comfortable pair of shoes. My sister had her own idea about what she thought I should have and was of no help. I saw a man standing behind the counter and looked at him for help. He said, "Picking out shoes is a very individual thing. Tell me a little about your situation." He was very nice, smiled, and seemed like he genuinely enjoyed selling shoes. He said he would bring me what I asked for and, if it was okay with me, a couple of additional items that might be suitable as well. "Of course!" I said. I ended up going with the more expensive item. He showed that he knew what he was talking about, knew his inventory and also knew how women bought. He was also enthusiastic!

Dale Carnegie said you can make more friends in two months by becoming really interested in other people than you can in two years by trying to get other people interested in you. It's true! It also reminds me of the adage:

People like people who like them.
People like people who think like them.
People like people who they think like them.
People like you if you like them.

Action steps

- Overhaul your customer communication program; how can it be enhanced?

Date for review:

Chapter 8

MAKE A GOOD FIRST IMPRESSION

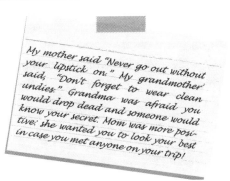

My mother said "Never go out without your lipstick on." My grandmother said, "Don't forget to wear clean undies." Grandma was afraid you would drop dead and someone would know your secret. Mom was more positive: she wanted you to look your best in case you met anyone on your trip!

You've probably heard plenty enough already on the topic of first impressions, but it bears repeating – especially when it's so easy for us to discredit ourselves in front of a customer.

So let's start with attire. When was the last time you updated your workplace attire? Have you added anything new? Could "old" be new? Check the Salvation Army and thrift stores for ideas. Vintage clothing can put a zip in your wardrobe. Seriously.

If you're selling fashionable merchandise, you should look like you understand fashion and color. Dress in a manner that is suitable for your workplace.

> **What people notice when they first meet you:**
>
> - Appearance and body language: 55%
> - Tone of voice: 38%
> - What you say: 7%
>
> Source: Image Talks, LLC

If you work in an upscale clothing store, it would not be wise to show up to work in ripped jeans and a tank top. Try wearing some of the clothing you're selling. This, again, shows your customers that not only do you want to sell this product to them, but it's good enough that you even want to wear it yourself. This is also a way to give them that first-person perspective that is so important.

Personally, I don't care for matching shirts with the name of the store embroidered on it. It reminds me of a bunch of kindergarteners on a field trip. Put yourself in someone else's shoes and imagine what their first thoughts of you would be. Is this what you'd want them to be? If not, you need to make the necessary changes.

When customers enter the store, do you rise out of your chair to meet them or do you stay seated?

Don't slouch, or lean against counters. Stand up and look proud, pull in your stomach muscles. It will help you look better – and build strong abs at the same time!

Use a firm handshake and look the person straight in the eye. Offer your hand to both male and female customers. I often hear that salespeople are uncertain about whether to shake a female customer's hand. It's always good manners to offer your hand. If the customer doesn't want to shake it, they won't.

If you're not sure about your handshake, test it out with other employees. If they say you have either a "bone crusher" grip or a "dead fish" grip, change it.

Look at your shoes. They may be fun or funny looking, but do they have a place on your selling floor?

Men: pull up your pants, get a pair of dress shoes and add only a touch of cologne, if any. Don't slather it on – you want to be seen, not smelled.

Women: I'm amazed when I see women who don't wear make-up. Just a little bit goes a long way and shows your customers that you have fashion sense. You don't have to look like a clown.

Treat your customers like royalty. Act as if they're all fascinating and have a million dollars to spend. You're not looking to waste any time though, and you're not looking for a date. If you don't know what to say, just stick with the basics of your product or your service.

The Value of a Smile

I once asked a class of fourth-graders to "define a smile." There were lots of interesting responses, but the best one came from a girl who said, "It's when you get the corners of your mouth to touch your ears."

This is, in my view, the closest anyone has ever come to explaining what a smile looks like and how it's achieved.

A smile is important in business, but some people dole them out as if they were rationed. If you pay your staff to smile, you might as well teach them to do it right. Find the salesperson with the most winning smile, videotape it and teach it to the rest of your staff. Now you can count how many times they do it and you can pay them "per smile." Sounds silly, but basically this is what you're doing when you pay your salespeople.

Remember, you're always creating first impressions. On your day off, think about how you look to your customers when you're "off duty." Is it that much different than when you're working? You want to be professional and friendly always!

Be personable, curious, and interested in the world around you. Your experiences, remember, help shape much of your personality. The more of them you have, the more of it you'll have.

Action steps

- What type of impression does your staff make?
- Give pointers to those willing to receive feedback on what they can do to improve how they affect the customer – or anyone.

Date for review:

Chapter 9

BE A PHONE WIZARD

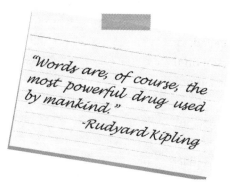

"Words are, of course, the most powerful drug used by mankind."

-Rudyard Kipling

The phone just might be one of the most valuable tools ever developed. When put in the right hands, it can lead to an inordinate amount of income. While plenty of business and communication is conducted online these days, the phone is still a critical factor in developing relationships, taking care of customers, and closing sales.

When answering the phone, answer with a smile. As silly as it may sound, the person on the other end can tell. Try it! A smile slows down your speech and makes you sound more personable. Call your own voicemail and see how it sounds; ask others what they think of your greeting.

Also, when answering the phone, be sure and use your name; for example: "Hi, this is Lis! How may I help you?"

Connecting on the phone really is an art. You might be someone who hangs up the second a telemarketer calls. I did too—until I did some consulting for a friend's telemarketing company. I learned firsthand how hard it was for salespeople to keep someone on the phone, and what skill was involved. Those who had mastered it, however, were amazing. Nowadays, I listen when a telemarketer calls. I also try to get them off track to see how capable they are at taking control of the conversation again. The good ones sound friendly, know their stuff and can deviate from the script. In fact, I try to listen to *anyone* making a pitch—from the religious folks to FedEx. They are all trying to do the same thing: connect to customers. Why not try to learn from them?

If you're making a call, be sure to state who you are, where you're calling from, and your reason for the call. Don't leave a message simply saying, "Give me a call" without giving some information about why you called.

Tell the person on the other end of the phone that you'll only take a moment, and ask if now's a good time.

Again, if you are making the call, make sure you've caught the person at a good time. Ask them, "Do you have a moment?" as opposed to just assuming they do.

If you need to place someone on hold, ask them if it's okay with them before doing so.

When you receive a call and the caller doesn't identify himself, asking "May I ask who's calling?" goes a lot further than, "Who's this?" If you've been asked to screen calls, explain to customers that the person is in a meeting and has asked for the names of any callers so he can get back to them quickly.

Be sure to write their name down. Pronounce the name and even ask for the spelling if necessary. Mary and John are rare these days – but Allex and Wynter aren't.

If you're going to put people on hold, give them a reasonable time frame. Remember, a moment is not always a moment.

Speak clearly. Make sure the person on the other end of the line can not only hear you, but can understand you as well. If you leave a message and haven't received a return call in a few hours or especially that day, call to make sure they got the message. The same applies for when you receive messages. Calling back within four hours is timely, a week later isn't.

Never answer the phone with anything in your mouth – that should be a given. Also, aim to answer the phone on the second ring. Answering on the first ring does, in fact, make you come across as too eager!

Writing a script is always an excellent idea. This can be for both outbound calls and inbound calls. This way everyone will know what to say – and while you don't have to stick to it religiously, it does offer guidance.

When you're finished with a phone call, thank the person for his or her time. "Thank you so much!" and "Have a great day!" are always nice to hear.

How about your voicemail message? I get a kick out of people who say they'll get back to me at their earliest convenience – it makes me feel real special. Leave a nice closing message on your voicemail, such as "I hope you're having a beautiful day," is a nice touch.

Oh, and skip the religious references.

Action steps

- Assess your staff's current skills and ability on the phone. How can they be improved?
- What books and literature do you have in-office that staff can use to improve their phone skills?

Date for review:

Chapter 10

MIND YOUR MANNERS

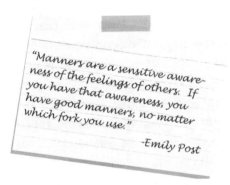

"Manners are a sensitive awareness of the feelings of others. If
you have that awareness, you
have good manners, no matter
which fork you use."

-Emily Post

Minding one's manners requires so little but leaves such a great impression, that it's mind-boggling more people aren't aware of what goes into this art. If we teach our kids to say "please," "excuse me" and "thank you," why would we not hold ourselves to the same standard?

If you know someone's last name, call them Mr. or Ms. (LAST NAME). If you don't know their last name call them "Sir" or "Miss" or simply ask what they prefer to be called. Many women nowadays don't want to be called "Ma'am" as it makes them feel too old! On the other hand, you can't assume they're married, so that cuts out "Mrs."

In short, the safest bet is to simply call them "Miss."

Manners aren't just about the niceties you express; they're also about your sensitivity to your environment.

I was completing a focus group once and one of the participants brought up an incident about a couple of salespeople he'd come across in a store. He described them as very competitive with each other, and it became clear they didn't like "sharing" customers from one department to another.

Apparently, the salespeople didn't think the customer noticed.

Remember, you are always on display. Customers notice who you're talking to and probably know everything you've said. So limit your conversations with co-workers while in front of customers. If you've got personal issues to discuss, discuss them somewhere else or at another time.

Do something that wouldn't be expected. If you see someone struggling in your store, go over and offer to help them carry something. I remember being in a retail tile store and watching as a customer carried out a huge – and very heavy – order. While the salesperson was standing in the doorway waving goodbye, a colleague – who happened to be female – ran out and helped the customer carry the tiles to the car. Now that's service!

In an age where it seems that manners are dwindling, be the one to set the example. Get your store known as the one with the really great service. Good manners go a long way towards reaching great customer service. It was Emily Post who said, "Manner is personality – the outward manifestation of one's innate character and attitude toward life."

GET TO KNOW ALL KINDS OF PEOPLE

Appreciate that there are differences in all people. Hey, the whole world is your backyard. There are different types of people with different customs and ideas. Examine what your stereotypes might be and how this may impact the way you treat certain customers.

Put yourself in a situation where you are forced to deal with your insecurities about people. Don't like the way that customer is dressed or how others spoke to you? Get perspectives from other people. Usually, it's our own biases that are creating the problem.

Is there a certain culture you're curious about? Go online. Read up on it. The saying is old, but it is true: Knowledge is power.

As I do sales training, I often hear salespeople talk about "those types" of people and what they're like. This predisposes that everyone thinks alike. While there may be similar trends and generalizations about people, not everyone is alike. You'll learn this the more you interact with the people, group or culture in question. You may feel out of place, but you can be sure you're not the only person ever to have felt this. It's good to get out of your comfort zone and learn new things. This doesn't mean you have to do this every day, but try it once and see how it goes. You never know, you may find some new things that you just love.

My accountant attends Chinese language classes with his young adopted child. It's given him the chance to learn and possibly even network in a different environment.

From my own personal experience, I've found that people love to share where they're from, and feel flattered that someone would be interested enough to ask. This opens the door to allow you to ask other questions about them or their culture.

The more we embrace differences, the more we'll grow and have a better appreciation for the diversity of the planet.

I remember being in the hospital with my friend who was in early labor. She was clearly stressed about the coming labor and wanted all the assurances in the world that things would go smoothly. The doctor walked in and was sweet as could be. He even had a cherubic face and an adorable accent. However, when he spoke she had a difficult time understanding him, which I could sense was a bit disconcerting for her. My friend just went ahead and broke the ice by asking: "Do you mind if I ask you something that is completely unrelated to medicine?" He looked a little perplexed, but said, "Sure." So she asked him where he was from. He brightened and said he came from Poland. Fascinated, we barraged him with questions about his life in Poland, and then in America, what made him decide to come here, whether he missed his homeland, etc. He was so pleasant and seemed genuinely excited to talk about it.

People love to talk about themselves. When I come across someone who's curious about me, I feel flattered. I can guarantee you that the best salespeople are often some of the most inquisitive. They're people who want to learn and grow, and they don't fear that someone will tell them to mind their own business!

Learn People's Names

When you learn someone's name, you immediately think differently of them. Why do you think this is?

In many ways, a name removes a barrier between individuals and humanizes each and every one of us. It helps to create a connection. In hostile court cases, prosecutors will often refer to a defendant as nothing more than "defendant," while the opposing counsel will always refer to his client by name. It reminds the jury that he is a person.

Addressing people by their name is respectful and shows that you have an interest in them. If you don't know someone's name, a good way to find out (other than bluntly asking it) is to introduce yourself first, and then pause to allow them to respond.

If you have a customer in your store and have momentarily forgotten their name, don't yell across the store, "Hey! I found that sample!" Just go up to them and tell them that you are so embarrassed but their name has just slipped out of your mind. They'll tell you again, and it's not a big deal. However, if you do this consistently, they might start to think you're just not listening. Which would be true!

Have you ever walked into a store and had the staff greet you by name? It's such a nice feeling. It also takes you by surprise – in a good way!

I remember walking around in Home Depot one day with a friend. We walked up to the paint counter and the clerk looked up and said to my friend, "Hi Shawn, welcome back." I was completely dumbfounded. Maybe my friend spends more time at Home Depot than I thought. Or maybe the employee simply takes the time to learn the names of customers.

A great way to remember a name upon learning it is to repeat it several times in your head, and then associate it with something about the person: "Rosalie wears a red sweater," for example. If the name is odd, ask for the spelling or pronunciation. Write it down if you need to.

I visit the Vietnamese nail shop near where I live and everyone has an Americanized name. I find it so much better when they use their real names though – it's so much more authentic. Everyone knows there are no Kathys in Vietnam!

Action steps

- Assess your current strengths and weaknesses in this area.
- Who stands out in your mind as someone with impeccable manners?
- How can you adopt these skills for both you and your staff?

Date for review:

Chapter 11

LEARN AND LISTEN WITH YOUR HEART

"To listen well is as powerful a means of communi-
cation and influence as
to talk well."

- John Marshall

When a customer is talking to you, listen not only to what they're saying, but to what they're not saying.

Listening isn't just about hearing, it's about watching as well. As we've said before, so much more is said through body language than through speaking.

Make sure your customers know you're listening to them. Give them signs such as nodding your head. Verbally indicate that you're listening, and use eye contact.

The customers will know you're listening if you ask them a question about what they've just said. Repeat what they've just said and ask about it. For example, if they've just told you they're looking for a mirror, you can respond with, "Of course! So I can have a better idea of what to show you, what room do you plan to put the mirror in?" Now they not only know you listened to them, but also know that you're not going to waste their time showing them a bunch of stuff they probably don't want to see.

Don't interrupt. Let the customers finish what they're saying before you jump in.

Stop trying to think of 50 different ways to answer this person's question while it's being asked. If you're doing that, you're not listening!

Don't finish people's sentences for them. Being cut-off in mid-sentence can be extremely annoying, not only in customer service but in every day life. You're not in that big of a rush are you? So let people finish their thoughts.

As the saying goes, "Don't judge a book by its cover." You can't assume a person's question is more or less important based on the way they look.

Lastly, give the customer your full attention. Don't start doing other tasks and giving them the occasional "uh huh" while doing so, as if this signals to them that you're listening. No. What this signals to them is that what they're saying to you right now is not important enough for you to stop what you're doing for one minute to listen to them.

Always make it about them.

Action steps

- How do you rate your listening skills?
- Make it a habit over the next week to listen more than you speak.

Date for review:

Chapter 12

FIND A WAY TO GIVE IT TO THEM

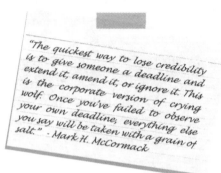

"The quickest way to lose credibility is to give someone a deadline and extend it, amend it, or ignore it. This is the corporate version of crying wolf. Once you've failed to observe your own deadline; everything else you say will be taken with a grain of salt." - Mark H. McCormack

If someone comes into your store knowing what they want, but you don't have it right now, you must find a way to get it. If it's impossible to get (i.e. it's no longer made or the brand isn't sold at your store anymore) show the customer that you'll go the extra mile to try and get it there.

When I travel, my drink of choice is an iced coffee blended with skim milk and three ice cubes. By some of the responses I've received, you would have thought I was making the most inane request in the world. People have objected by saying it's against the Board of Health's rules to put milk in the blender (which may of course be valid—but shouldn't you wash it after each use anyway?), that the process is too involved or even, incredibly, that it's not going to taste right. I think I know my own tastes!

Most people know what they want when they walk into your store, but a lot of the time they might be hesitant to buy, due to cost or simple uncertainty.

Listen to your customer and figure out which category they fall under and then proceed accordingly.

Put your opinions aside. Your customers may come in and request something that you wouldn't wish on your worst enemy.

That's okay. It's not your decision; it's theirs, so give it to them! If they ask your opinion you can let them know, nicely, that though it may not have been your first choice, it's something that you're sure they'll enjoy. You don't want to lie to your customers, but there's also no need to let them know that you think their taste is hideous! There's a tasteful way to say almost anything.

There are also useful ways to deal with customers who need items in a hurry. If, say, you work in a jewelry store and this customer needs a repair done, but they're going away so they need it done today, get on the phone with the jewelry repair person and let him know that you've got a very important client who needs something done immediately. This will make the customer feel extra special. If the typical time for a repair return is two weeks, and you've just been told that he can get it back to you in three days, well, that's quite remarkable. However, this still may not be good enough for the client.

Try to turn over every stone for your customer. If the quickest time is three days, then let them know that you've done everything you can, and you will call them personally when their item is in, but that three days is the soonest it can be done. They may walk away frustrated, but at least they've seen that you've done everything that you could to make this happen, and in the end it should make them feel a little better. If it doesn't, there's nothing you can do, and you've done your best. Hey, you can't please everyone!

Action steps

- Write down a time where someone went out of their way to help you. How could you do the same for someone else?

Date for review:

Chapter 13

Speak Well of Everyone

"Make it a habit to tell people thank you. To express your appreciation, sincerely and without the expectation of anything in return. Truly appreciate those around you, and you'll soon find many others around you. Truly appreciate life, and you'll find that you have more of it." -Ralph Marston

Speak well of everyone you know, and everyone you come into contact with. This should begin with your fellow employees! Thank them for the job they're doing, because if it weren't for all of them, you wouldn't have a store.

When your employees have earned it, brag about them in front of customers when given the opportunity. This gives customers a good feeling about you, the business and the team. In some ways, when you brag about them you are also indirectly bragging about yourself.

If one employee is really shining and taking the reins, do something so they know you've noticed. Mention it at a staff meeting, leave a note on their desk or add a little bonus in their check.

When it comes time for the holidays, remember not only your customers and employees, but also the countless other people who help keep your business running. The mailman, UPS guy, delivery drivers, vendors, etc. It's always nice to recognize people for their work, even if it's just a thank-you card.

Don't Take People for Granted

Taking people or things for granted can only lead to disappointment. If someone goes above and beyond in her job, and you come to expect that of her, you'll be in for disappointment when the day comes when she doesn't do it. Also, you may start to hold her to standards that may not even be in her job description.

A photographer friend, Katie, has a son who plays football. Naturally, she brings her camera to every game. Since she's always snapping away, she gets shots of other kids on the team as well. One day she decided to send off a couple of these pictures to the coach, who thought they were excellent and asked if she would show the parents. Well, the parents loved them so much that Katie started taking more and more pictures at every game and then e-mailing them to the parents. As a gift to the coaches, she thought it would be nice to get the whole team together for a group picture. She did all of this at no charge, and was happy to do it because people were so appreciative of it. Katie happens to be a little too giving sometimes, in my opinion, but hey, to each her own! She made people happy, and that's what allowed her to continue to want to do it.

One day, a mother of one of the other football kids asked if Katie would provide some advice on class picture day at the school. From what she was told, all she would have to do would be to show up to a meeting or two and give her input. That's not how it went though. She ended up being the only person who showed up at the meeting. The woman who was supposed to be in charge didn't even show.

Apparently, the other woman thought Katie was going to take on the whole project. Considering how close it was to class picture day, she felt she had no other option but to take care of it, otherwise the kids wouldn't have their pictures taken.

Nowadays, Katie is not so quick to just go and do things for free. She learned the hard way that there might be someone willing to take advantage of it.

The next year my friend's son moved up in football, so she was no longer involved with the same parents or the same coach. As she was leaving practice with her son one evening, some of the parents from the prior year saw her and rushed up to her, saying, "Oh we miss you

so much! Your pictures were so great. Please come back to our team!
We want you back!"

This recognition and thanks was all she needed to make her feel
on top of the world again.

You never know how far a simple "thank you" goes until you
receive a sincere one.

Action steps

- Visit your library for a copy of "The Power of Positive
  Thinking," by Dr. Norman Vincent Peale
- Write down three positive characteristics of anyone you've
  ever found to be difficult.

Date for review:

PART II

MEASURE IT TO MAKE IT HAPPEN

Chapter 14

CREATE BENCHMARKS FOR SUCCESS

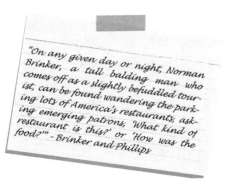

"On any given day or night, Norman Brinker, a tall balding man who comes off as a slightly befuddled tourist, can be found wandering the parking lots of America's restaurants, asking emerging patrons, 'What kind of restaurant is this?' or 'How was the food?'" - Brinker and Phillips

If you ask a salesperson what he does for a living, he'll say, "I sell." If you ask him what that means, he'll probably scratch his head for a moment before offering a vague definition.

In order to quantify and improve upon something, you must first be able to define it. Only then will you have a benchmark on which to compare future results.

BENCHMARKING

What is benchmarking? Benchmarking is a fancy way of finding out what people do that works, and then standardizing it.

Training your staff without having any measurable benchmarking standards in place is pretty much a waste of time. For one thing, how will you know whether people are improving, and then how will you be able to measure your return on investment?

Let's say your most successful salespeople are the ones who ask for referrals immediately after a sale. Once you've identified that as the differentiating factor in your staff's success, you can start measuring other's performances.

You don't have to reinvent the wheel. Your outstanding employees already know what works – they're way ahead of the game.

Focus on other areas, such as delivering excellent customer service. If we can get everyone to deliver outstanding service, the customers will love you and you'll be on the road to success.

I worked with a successful retailer once who asked me to interview all of their peak performers. After just a few interviews, it was very apparent that the peak performers didn't care about the bad economy or anything that was "outside" their control. Instead, they focused on what they knew worked and did more of it. We ascertained that focus, goal-setting and an interest in self-improvement were deciding factors in who became a peak performer and who didn't.

Keep an eye out for those who deliver excellent results and who do the right thing. Be a detective: Watch the behaviors, dissect the behaviors and ask questions. There's no downside to testing each employee from time to time on his or her abilities. In fact, it's a *must* in sales!

A stockbroker friend of mine started out as a sales assistant making cold calls for a broker. He made calls from 9-6 every day and had a huge amount of pressure placed on him to perform. Every week, he went in front of the sales manager to be tested on his phone skills. The manager would play the part of the prospect on the other end of the phone and throw every sort of objection possible at the young sales assistant. As a result of these high-pressure situations in front of his boss, the sales assistant went on to became a highly-successful financial advisor.

As a way to improve employee performance while boosting customer satisfaction, you might consider recording your employees as they receive calls from customers. Disclose this to both parties if you plan to go ahead. The customers will appreciate the level of quality control. Your staff – if they want to excel – will welcome the feedback. Granted, feedback is not always comfortable. At golf school I shuddered whenever my coach said he was going to video my swing. Why? Because I knew I was going to learn just how bad I really was. My coach, however, focused plenty on what I did right – not just the areas I did wrong. He said with great enthusiasm, "See that swing?

Look at your grip and your movement. Let's analyze that so you can do it every time." There was positive reinforcement and encouragement.

THE IMPORTANCE OF REFERRALS

Statistics say that by the time your business is five years old, 80% of your customers will be referrals. It must be a great feeling when business owners realize they have enough happy customers that they no longer have to advertise for business.

A referral tells you the customer likes the way you deliver the goods and is happy to tell a friend. Sure, there are plenty of customers who may be happy with what you do but not interested in referring anyone — but their numbers are few. Everyone knows someone who'd be interested in what you provide. It might take the customer a day or two, but if you stay on him he'll come up with a name.

When I was in the flooring business, I remember one of my sales reps asking a customer, "Do you know anyone who might benefit from my expertise?" The customer thought for a moment and said, "No one that I can think of, but my brother is drawing up plans for a four unit apartment house."

Everyone has someone to refer, they just might not realize it.

QUANTIFYING YOUR CUSTOMER SERVICE PLAN

So what are the components of your customer service plan? Is it referrals, a glowing letter, "Raving Fans" (as Ken Blanchard put it), or high ratings? Can you take these to the bank? If you don't define it and follow up, how will you know if it has been delivered?

A good measure of customer service is how willing your customers are to help you build your business. Make it quantifiable.

Require your employees to ask customers if their question or concern was adequately answered or resolved. Then, provide the means for your customers to rate your employees on customer service.

One of the most effective ways to do this is to hand out, mail or e-mail a feedback form to which customers can easily respond. Offer an incentive for them to fill it out.

Make sure everyone is focused on customer service by hiring mystery shoppers. That way, the complacent employees will be forced to stay on their toes. If you don't constantly monitor your employees, how will you know if what they're doing is helping your business?

Remember, sales numbers are not always a good measurement for determining if the salesperson is delivering good customer service. Businesses tend to put up with employees who keep sloppy paperwork, don't call back customers and don't follow up. They focus on short term goals – such as how much money the person will bring in this week – as opposed to what will sustain the business over the long term.

I knew a salesperson who had great numbers and seemed to be very nimble at closing customers. After about three months, however, it became known that he was lying to them. His game was to completely and utterly flatter his customer. He didn't care so much whether the sale was even in the buyer's best interest. Not everyone fell for it, but those who did ended up feeling betrayed, and it caused irreparable harm to the business.

Build good customer service by monitoring your employees, what they're selling and how they're selling it. This way you can create standards for good work.

In the words of Mary Case: "No pressure, no diamonds."

Action steps

- How will you collect benchmarking standards for your business?
- Do you have training in place?

Date for review:

Chapter 15

DEVELOP FOCUS THROUGH A MISSION

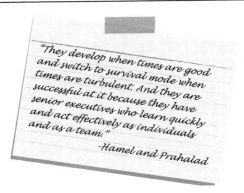

"They develop when times are good and switch to survival mode when times are turbulent. And they are successful at it because they have senior executives who learn quickly and act effectively as individuals and as a team."

–Hamel and Prahalad

Do you ever have a difficult time getting started?

My friend Geno has a health club and in January the regulars complain about all the new people in line behind the treadmills, intent on fulfilling their New Year's resolutions. Geno doesn't worry about it, because he knows something that most of us don't: The new people crowding the treadmills won't last. They'll work out for a few days and then go back to their old habits. Geno's seen it a thousand times already. Sure enough, two weeks into the New Year, the gym is back to normal and the regulars have ready access to the treadmills.

Too many people talk about doing stuff and never do it. There's nothing more boring than listening to people brag about what you know they're not going to do. In 1988, Nike and Dan Wieden came up with the famous tagline, "Just do it." The slogan is considered to be one of the top five ads of the 20th century. Why? Because it's brief, direct, motivating, and you simply can't argue with it!

Being focused means different things to different people. In many ways, what you focus on is what you become. So the question is: What do you want your business to become? Even though fat people often claim they don't know what they ate to get fat, I would surmise it's probably fatty foods!

In order for you to "Just do it," or to simply "do the right thing," you first have to know what *it* or *the right thing* is. This is where your mission comes in.

YOUR MISSION

You've heard of a mission statement before. A mission statement answers the question of who you are and why you're doing what you're doing.

Remember the saying that started circulating around my dad – "Once Tony's customer, always Tony's customer"? Well, that became a part of his mission statement. Once you became one of Tony's customers, he practically never let you out of his sight. When he found a good customer, one that had money and paid his bills, Tony held on to them. His aim was to provide excellent service and to retain his customers.

Your mission is what you believe and it captures the essence of why you started the business in the first place.

STANDARDIZE YOUR MISSION

If good customer service is your goal, then the way you go about it needs to be consistent and standardized. You start with your mission statement and then standardize it by making it something you believe in.

Every business came from a dream, an idea, a place you wanted to go and where you wanted the business to be.

The dream is what you strive for; the mission statement puts it on paper and tells you how you're going to get there. It's like writing the words for a song – words make the song come alive.

Write a company statement that captures the essence of who you are, but isn't so vague and generalized that it could apply to every other company out there. It should focus the energies of the whole organization – and your customers too – in a purposeful way.

Consider the following mission statement from Southwest Airlines:

> Southwest Airlines is dedicated to the highest quality of Customer Service delivered with a sense of warmth, friendliness, individual pride, and Company Spirit.

I thought about how this fit when, in 2008, American Airlines flights were temporarily grounded because of safety concerns. Destined for one of those flights were young musicians scheduled to play for a group of very important people in the Midwest. As the story goes, the kids were stranded and upset because they wouldn't have the opportunity that they'd been rehearsing for. Southwest ended up loading the kids on one of their planes and flying them to their destination so they could make their debut. Not because American asked them to, but because Southwest saw it as an opportunity to provide the highest quality of customer service in their industry.

So ask yourself, does your mission statement encapsulate the best of who you are and who you want to be? Does it engage the emotions? It should bring tears to your eyes and joy to your heart. It's why you get up in the morning and it is what you think about when you have a conflict with a customer – you ask yourself, "How can I stay true to my mission while resolving this conflict?"

It must be ambitious yet simple and practical. Not everyone can be President of the United States in their lifetime, but everyone can strive to become a leader in some form or another. Make it practical.

It should also make sense to everyone. It is the basis of your company. Everyone in your business should understand what the business means and want to make it happen.

It should be written, posted somewhere where you'll see it often and read periodically.

Be proud of your mission.

Read it at your meetings and special events. Think of it as the National Anthem for your business, or the Pledge of Allegiance.

Put it on everyone's desk so they are reminded of why they're doing what they're doing.

You can't fake your mission – it's the essence of who you are.

SLOGANS AND STATEMENTS

The clearer and more direct you are in your mission, your purpose or your vision, the better off you'll be. Consider these statements from some of the biggest names in a variety of industries:

- **Walmart**: To help people save money so they can live better.
- **American Red Cross**: To improve the quality of human life; to enhance self-reliance and concern for others; and to help people avoid, prepare for, and cope with emergencies.
- **Dell**: To be the most successful computer company in the world at delivering the best customer experience in markets we serve.
- **Save the Whales**: To educate children and adults about marine mammals, their environment and their preservation.
- **Green & Black's**: To create the most delicious chocolate in a manner that helps sustain life on our precious planet.
- **McDonald's**: To be the world's best quick service restaurant experience.

These mission statements don't simply focus on one tiny detail, but encapsulate a broad vision. McDonald's, for example, doesn't say anything about creating a perfect hamburger. The pursuit of the perfect "quick service" hamburger simply helps them stay on task in their mission. Their mission helps keep their employees focused on the greater objective of the company. A mission is something you *adhere to*.

If I were a McDonald's employee, it wouldn't necessarily be the best place for me to showcase my Italian roots. I wouldn't add tomato sauce to a Big Mac because I felt it needed it, or even because some of my customers liked it. That wouldn't be upholding McDonald's mission statement. Instead, I would strive to keep to the company's principles as best I could, and if I felt there wasn't a match, I'd be out looking for new employment.

You may already have a mission statement in place, or at least a semblance of a mission statement. Take some time to think about it and decide whether it's still on target. When you have this completed, write down your mission statement here:

_____

_____

_____

_____

_____

Once you know your mission, everything about your business flows from there. Without it, you're playing cards in the dark. Only if someone opens the door to let some light in do you know anything about what you're doing. The mission opens the door for you and your business.

One note: It's not only businesses that thrive on mission statements, but individuals too. If you're an employee, entrepreneur or student, identifying a mission statement will help guide you on your path to success.

Your next step, then, is to develop your course of action and to make sure everyone's on board with you, following it to the letter. No ifs, ands or buts about it. McDonalds decides what needs to be done, standardizes the process and then focuses on getting it done. Standardizing is a way of measuring.

If you can't measure it, you can't tell if you're doing it right.

Action steps

- Write your mission statement or, if you have one, review it to see if it still fits with your values.
- How is the mission carried out in your business?

Date to review:

Chapter 16

STRIVE TO BE DIFFERENT

In 2008, Converse celebrated 100 years in the shoe business. Over the years, the company has immersed itself in pop culture - from 1976's smash hit "Rocky," in which Sly Stallone trained in his black Converse, to 2006's Harry Potter and the Order of the Phoenix. The company knows how to keep up with the times, while retaining its signature style.

What can you do to be different? Those companies that weather the test of time have shown that they have a product that sells. While Converse has provided the same style shoe over several decades, their marketing efforts around the product have kept the shoe fresh in our minds. After 100 years, the shoe is still seen as hip and modern.

Consider these ideas to help spruce up your product or service.

Paint your place – both inside and out. Does your store need a new paint job? You'd be surprised at how much a coat of paint can do for a store. If your customer is female, think how often she changes styles. My guess is it's with the seasons: four times a year. Look at restaurants and bars. Every few years they change their interiors and even their names.

According to statistics on stores that do "redos," traffic increases immediately after the redo. Why? Because customers want to see what's new and different. Your upgrade makes you look prosperous.

Reinvent yourself. Are you familiar with the story of Godiva, the Belgian chocolate company? On the verge of bankruptcy, so it goes, the company decided it had nothing to lose by tripling its prices and reinventing itself as one of the most posh candy companies in the world. Look where they are now.

How about some new products designed to make you look cutting edge? Every year, Neiman Marcus comes out with super expensive Christmas gifts – ones that only a very few can afford. They've become known for this. Now, if someone wants something new and exciting and has lots of dollars to spend, they know where to go.

Keep your customers guessing. What could you do to keep customers guessing around the holidays? Bring in a Santa Claus, give away Christmas trees, celebrate Chanukah and Kwanzaa. Bring in items you've never carried before and surprise your customers.

Keep up on the latest trends in your industry. Talk with your suppliers in order to find out what's new. Can you plan an event and invite your good customers to see the new stuff? In the "olden days" the vendors called it a trunk show.

See what your competitors are doing. Go to stores that sell items similar to yours and see what they're doing. Vow to do something different. Don't just copy them or try to one-up them. If they have the exact same items you have, throw them out and get different stuff. If you all have the same merchandise, the one with the cheapest price will win. You don't want to win that game.

Read as many trade magazines as you can. Read what's new rather than what's being done time after time. It's been said that if you read one hour a day in your field, in five years you will be considered an expert.

Read magazines from other trades as well. What are they doing to stay ahead of the competition? If your customer is female, go down to the cosmetics counter in the local department store and see how things are being sold. Check out Sephora or the Body Shop – what are they doing? Go out of your industry and look for trends.

Spruce up your store and your advertising. See what can be used to spruce up the message you're putting out there. What are the national companies doing? What are the themes and how do they compare to your industry? Out of all the insurance company ads, Nationwide Insurance seems to have the commercials that make the most sense. They show real life problems that most of us can relate to, but they do it in a humorous way. I think of one particular ad in which a couple is driving in a convertible. The man is obviously quite taken with his companion. As they drive, the woman's scarf comes from around her neck and wraps around the driver's eyes, creating pandemonium. You watch in horror as he tries to remove the scarf, but before he can, they drive through a field and the car coasts (harmlessly) into a tree. The voice in the background reminds us: "Life comes at you fast."

Well, *I* found it funny.

Be known as the store that's always trying to do right by the customer. What's right, you say? It's whatever provides the best experience for the customer while upholding your mission statement.

If you do it "real right," have the customer provide a testimonial saying that you did.

BE ALWAYS CHANGING

There's a great book written in the late '80s (and revised in 2002) called *Customers for Life* by Carl Sewell. Carl took over his father's Cadillac business and the first thing he did was to look at the revenue. He realized that most of the revenue came from service rather than sales, and that their garage was open from 9-5, Monday through Friday. He also learned that customers averaged seven Cadillacs during the course of their lifetime. Wow! Armed with this knowledge, Carl extended the hours of the garage through the evenings, and went so far as to open up the business on Saturdays – which was practically unheard of then. He was so successful that when Lexus started taking over the wealthier Cadillac customers, they came to Sewell to discuss his managing a Lexus dealership.

Change is inevitable, so embrace it! When we look back to the "good ole days," it seems so many businesses spent energy on *not changing*. Businesses, in fact, tried to *control* the market rather than adapt to it – it was common for stores not to buy from suppliers if the shop down the street sold the same goods and discounted them. There was also plenty of price-fixing going on in those days as well.

One of the duties in my first job at a clothing store in Washington, D.C. was to spy on my competitors and ensure that we were matching the same high prices. It didn't matter whether our inventory was worth it – it only mattered if we were being competitive with our competitors.

THINK OF YOURSELF AS A BUSINESS DOCTOR

My friend Stan has a vanity plate that says: BIZDOC. He calls himself the business doctor because the first thing he'll do for you, free of charge, is give your business a "fiscal." He checks out your business model, your staff, how you operate and then provides a diagnosis, which you can take or leave. You have to hire him to get the remedy, of course.

You may need to change quite a bit in order to ensure you're providing the best customer service and getting a leg up on the competition. Remember, if times are tight, there's probably only one customer shopping, and that's the one with money. The rest are staying home, turning off the lights and trying to figure out what to do next to save a dime. These aren't your customers. You're after the ones who still aren't afraid to spend a buck.

Expensive customers want expensive-looking stores. If the outside of your store doesn't look good, what kind of customers do you think it'll attract?

I find it interesting when owners find it *good* that customers are surprised at how nice the interior of their store is, compared to the exterior. These owners don't realize that if the store looked awful on the outside and customers still went in, it was probably because they were looking for a deal. Wealthy customers don't want to shop in stores that look like they won't be in business next month, so you need to evaluate what you can change in order to ensure you're attracting the best customers. In tight times, it might suit you to look as prosperous as possible.

Action steps

- Evaluate areas of your business that could use an upgrade.
- Write down any options you could use to change those areas.

Date to review:

Chapter 17

PRICE MERCHANDISE SO CUSTOMERS UNDERSTAND THE VALUE

"Mark the cheap things cheap and the expensive things expensive," Tony said. "That way customers don't get confused, nor will you!"

I once visited a store called The Spirit of the Red Horse, which you'll find in a number of airport terminals. There was a handbag priced at $450 sitting next to a roller bag three times as big priced at $477. I asked the clerk why the smaller bag was almost as much as the big bag and the clerk said it was because the smaller bag had more "bling" on it. I suggested he look up the cost because I was sure it was marked incorrectly – there really wasn't anything different from the bigger bag. He looked it up and said the pricing was right, though he couldn't pinpoint as to why. "It just is."

My thoughts: Either the handbag was priced too high or the roller bag was priced too low. There wasn't an obvious reason as to why these different items warranted a similar price.

Most retailers, in my experience, work on what they call a standard markup. They buy an item for $5, and sell it for $10. Or rather, they sell it for cheap. (They'll say it's "inexpensive," but I say it's "cheap.")

The ideal approach is to price things based on what people will spend. The value of an item, remember, is what someone is willing to pay for it. Don't price solely on how much you paid for it. Items that are new, have recognizable brand name or simply have features that make them *sell,* should command higher prices. If you work on a standard markup, the cheap stuff will probably look too expensive and the good stuff will look too cheap.

If one thing is selling well, up the price a little. If it keeps selling, up the price a little more. Keep doing this until the product isn't doing well, and then go back to what the price was when it was flying off the shelves. Though remember: If merchandise is selling too quickly, you're probably leaving money on the table!

If you're able to, get brand names. This will always pull in some new people while at the same time keeping the loyal customers interested. If you can't buy brand name merchandise directly from your supplier, buy it through other channels. Or buy higher quality items from second-tier names.

Purchase good off-brand or off-priced merchandise so you can put it on sale in your store. Let your customers know why this is a good buy, and compare the pros and cons of the product with its higher-priced competitors. Brand names make a difference in any industry. Your store brand will also make a difference.

Do something other places will not do, and market it.

Don't drop your prices because of temptation, poor cash flow or because of your next door neighbor. There are customers who want to brag that they can afford the best. Let them. I call this type of bragging a "wankism." No, that's not a bad word! Mrs. Wank was one of my father's lovely customers. One day mom took me to Mrs. Wank's house to show me the work dad had done. I noticed that Mrs. W. still had the price tags hanging from her chandeliers. As Mrs. W. took us through the house she not only pointed out the new features added to the house, she pointed out the prices strategically hanging from these features. When I asked my mom why Mrs. W. had done that, she said *because she can!*

Offer services that your customer can't get elsewhere. Do something special for your customer and let everyone know.

My supermarket will cut a loaf bread for you if you ask them, which I find incredibly valuable. Have you ever tried to slice a loaf of soft fresh bread? When I asked the market why they didn't advertise this service, they said because it's too much work! I would venture to say that they are working too hard doing things that aren't directly customer-focused. How many times did I *not* buy the loaf of bread because I had made such a mess of it when I got it home? This is a service that most baked goods stores offer, but no one knows about it because they don't market it. Make these things known!

Action steps

- Go over your inventory and determine whether the prices best reflect the product's value.
- Consider new ways to provide value to your customers.

Date to review:

Chapter 18

ACT IN YOUR OWN SELF INTEREST

Never underestimate one's motives. I read an old interview about Liz Taylor's marriage to Nicky Hilton. When asked what they had in common, Liz said, "We both like hamburgers." I asked my mother if that was enough reason to get married and she said, "People get married for less!"

Be inquisitive, look for new stuff, read magazines, go to the movies, watch the Academy Awards or a hockey game.

Don't get stuck in your industry.

Remember when your mom asked you, "If everyone jumped off the bridge would you jump too?" You said "no," but of course you didn't mean it. Being like everyone else in school made you popular. Being like everyone else in the retail business, however, will make you poor. Just because everyone is doing it doesn't make it right or wrong—it just *is*; but what makes you think you have to be like everyone else?

HE WHO HAS THE LOWEST PRICE LOSES

In retail, when everything is the same product and the same service, the lowest price wins. Except, no one really *wins*. Eventually, having the lowest price will just put you out of business – unless you're a mega-store like Walmart, which can afford to take significant losses in some areas.

There used to be a store called The Wiz whose tagline was, "Nobody Beats the Wiz!" While it was a cute slogan, it also guaranteed they would be out of business someday. They sold everything at the lowest price and then, one day, they were gone. Did the lowest prices do it? I don't know, but I can't help feeling their tagline prophesized their demise!

Keep Trying Different Angles

I know a carpet retailer who offers his customers "white glove installation." White glove means: no hassle; we'll keep everything clean and neat. His television spokesperson is an attractive woman who wears white gloves. People eat it up!

Do Something Good For Someone

Be part of the customer's life. Find a cause that's important to you and donate to it. Let the customer know that this is something new that you're doing. Offer them the chance to give to the cause as well, and then send them a thank-you card for doing so. Keep them informed as to how much you were able to raise and that your goal next year is to do even better! It's something different, and everyone loves to help.

I knew a retailer who had a "platinum club" for good customers. "Good" meant you spent a lot of money. Well, at Christmas time these customers were invited to help deliver gifts to the local nursing home and to go Christmas caroling. They also wrapped presents for Toys for Tots. He said they loved belonging!

Action steps

- Keep a list tracking how much money or time is spent on pursuits that don't serve your business.
- Come up with five new ways to modernize your business strategy

Date to review:

Chapter 19

RELENTLESSLY PURSUE CUSTOMER SATISFACTION

Many companies focus on beating the competition. When you think this way you will always be second best. You're letting your competition set the pace.

Successful companies are relentless in the pursuit of what their customers think about them and how they can use that feedback to their benefit. Relentless means providing the best customer experience before, during and after the buying process.

BEFORE

Take care to ensure that your store, Web site, products and services and staff are representative of your brand. Your customers will form their impression instantly. If there's "chatter" out there in the Web world about your service, make sure you're staying on top of it and addressing any problems that arise.

DURING

Let your customers know you're there to help them while they're shopping, but don't breathe down their necks. Chances are they won't buy now, but they likely will a few days from now. One thing that will guarantee their not coming back to you is a high-pressure selling environment. Seeing a salesperson visibly annoyed about a customer not purchasing something – no matter how long they've been in the store – will virtually guarantee they won't be back.

AFTER

There are plenty of ways to keep your store top-of-mind after a customer buys from you, and their feedback is invaluable. Consider these tips:

- If your job was at someone's house, leave a gift and make it something related to the job. I remember being in this cute store in Phoenix called *l'Orange*. There, I found a sink stopper with a man on the top with hands raised, as if he were saying, "Don't let me drown!" If you're in the kitchen business, wouldn't you think this a great gift for your customers?
- If you're in a store, have comment sheets available for the customers and a box for them to leave their replies in.
- Never ask the customer filling out a comment sheet to leave his or her name on it – who wants to be known as the person who left the bad comment? If you want their name on it you will need a special "lock box" that only you can view.
- If a mistake has been made, apologize immediately and make up for it tenfold. Don't wait to act on it too. This will not only make the customer feel good that you've recognized and admitted your mistake, but it will make doing business with you again a comfortable proposition. Always do the right thing for your customer.
- Hold an informal customer panel. I invited 25 couples for a wonderful dinner at one of my customer's stores. We explained that they had been invited because of their loyalty and their "investment" in our store. They were so touched!

They answered all our questions and said they would give whatever help we needed. You can't buy that kind of loyalty. If you decide to do this, make sure these customers know that they've been chosen because they are "special" customers, and give them little gifts for their time and effort in helping you.

- Find out what similar stores are doing – do you do what they do or do you do it better? Maybe you shouldn't do it at all!

Action steps

- Send out a survey to existing customers to gauge their happiness with your product and/or service.
- Come up with 10 new ways to improve customer satisfaction.

Date to review:

Chapter 20

MORE ON FEEDBACK

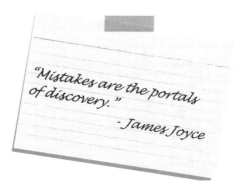

"Mistakes are the portals of discovery."

-James Joyce

You may have heard this already, but the message needs to be repeated: Constructive criticism will help you move forward faster than 1000 compliments. Too much criticism, on the other hand, will take away your self-confidence and leave you not wanting to play anymore.

It's not necessarily compliments that help to build self esteem; it's giving people sincere information that will help them do better and help them gain a better sense of self.

It seems that kids who grow up with constant praise and no critical feedback become adults who are afraid to listen to negative comments. If your job requires you to be in someone's house or store, leave a comment card with postage already on it. If you're at an on-site job, thank the client for their business and leave comment sheet ratings for you and your employees. Make it simple. Just ask the customer how they feel about your store, the service, the products, and how the job went.

Ask your customers what you could do to better the store. If they say "nothing," ask them what they would do if it were their store. If they still say "nothing," move on. You're not going to get anything more from them.

Ask your employees! What do they think of the products you (and they) are selling, and what is selling the most? What could you do without? Do they have any new ideas for the look of the store?

Telephone surveys can also be a handy tool. Write out a questionnaire and hire some college kids over the summer to go through your list of customers to see what they like and don't like. Make this a yearly thing. Many people don't like to do phone surveys, but if they hear it's from one of their favorite stores, they might be a little more willing to give in. I know I would.

Get a focus group together. Get all different ages and different genders, and add in a store employee or two. Now that you've got the perfect ingredients, mix it up and see what they think. Thank them for doing this, and give them a little thank-you gift.

Have your store mystery-shopped once a month. Get the feedback from your mystery shopper, and go over it with everyone who works in that store

Always know what the competitors are selling, and what's doing well for them. Mystery shop their store.

On your Web site, create a page exclusively for customer comments. Print out every negative one, and go over them with your employees to try and make it better. It wouldn't be a bad idea to pull a couple of good ones as well, and put them up in the store somewhere where other customers will be able to read them. This will also let you and your employees know that there are good things being done as well.

Give away some products to your valuable long-term customers along with an evaluation sheet. Ask them to test the products and return the evaluations in a week or two. You might get a couple of people who'll just take the products and run, but the ones who do fill out the form will be well worth it.

GIVING FEEDBACK TO YOUR EMPLOYEES

Feedback goes both ways: It can be used as praise or as a means of correcting behavior. Both approaches can be invaluable – particularly when used to correct behavior. Take care, however, as many people are sensitive to getting feedback. If you've noticed that an employee or even a co-worker has done something wrong, tell them in private and simply stick to the facts. There's no need for punishment outside of any usual consequences of poor performance.

Never reprimand someone in front of customers. It's like being yelled at by your mom in front of your friends. You don't have to be reminded how that felt. Wait for an appropriate time and an appropriate place to speak to them.

And remember, don't take people for granted; every task done well should be noticed. If you're an owner or manager, be there for your staff 24 hours a day. You probably won't get many calls, but it helps in the minds of those who might need you to know you're available.

Action steps

- Review your current approach to feedback. Are you and your employees open to it?
- Set up bi-monthly or quarterly reviews to determine how your staff is performing.

Date to review:

Chapter 21

STRATEGIES THAT MAKE A DIFFERENCE

"Anyone can make the simple complicated – creativity is making the complicated simple."
-Charles Mingus

Keep your promises – and then go beyond them. If your customer keeps visiting to see if an item has come in, offer to mail it to them on your dollar.

If someone is a regular customer, occasionally give them a discount. Even if the discount is the only 10%, the customer will still feel like they've won the lottery. It's unexpected and will certainly keep them coming back for more.

If you work directly in retail, offer to wrap gifts bought from your store at no charge. This is particularly valuable during the holiday season, though it'll also be welcome at any time of the year.

If your store is small enough, offer the customers tea or coffee. This is true for nicer hotels, so why not make it so for nicer businesses? Do something that sets you apart and makes people feel like you've put a little something extra into it for them.

Give people the unexpected, but while doing so make sure to continue giving them the expected as well.

Make your store an inviting environment so people will enjoy walking around.

Offer free shipping if possible.

I love shopping at Bath and Body Works because every time I go in there I get something for free. Well, I *think* I get something for free. Even if they make the prices higher on one item just so that we, as consumers, think we're getting another item for free, it makes me feel good. I've also never walked out of that store without having a coupon or two thrown in my bag. To me, this is giving more than what's expected, by far.

Remember, if we don't take care of our customers, someone else will.

Action steps

- What are your current business strategies to take care of your customers?
- Consider whether a coupon program is a good approach for your business.

Date to review:

Chapter 22

CLOSE YOUR SALES WITH POSITIVE REMARKS TO THE CUSTOMER

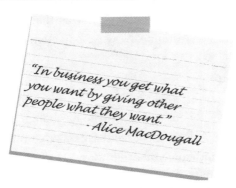

"In business you get what you want by giving other people what they want."
- Alice MacDougall

Everyone likes to hear something nice, something genuine. When closing a sale, thank the person for their time, and then compliment them on something that they wouldn't have expected (e.g. "By the way, that's a great jacket! Where'd you get it?"). This may seem a bit forced at first, but when you become practiced in this skill and genuine in your feeling, it comes across nicely to the customer.

You want to close a sale on a positive note or with a positive remark because you get the person's attention. By getting their attention in a good way, there's a likelier chance they'll leave your store feeling good. If they leave your store feeling good, it gives them that much more reason to come back again.

How many times have you been witness to someone buying something and not even looking at the salesperson? Or just grunting at them?

I went out to dinner with my friend one night to a restaurant that we'd been to many times. We had a new waitress that night, which put me on guard since our usual waitress already knew our likes and dislikes. So, this poor girl already had a strike against her, in my book, simply because she wasn't who I wanted her to be! At any rate, she came to our table to deliver us our water and our menus. As soon as she looked up to introduce herself she said, "Oh my gosh, I *love* your glasses!" She went on and on about them and it basically broke the ice for me. I started to laugh because though I liked my glasses, I'd never quite gotten this response! I thanked her and told her where I got them.   Needless to say, she got a nice tip from us. It wasn't so much that I needed to be complimented; it was that the compliment was unexpected and very genuine. Now we have two favorite waitresses!

Action steps

- Think of someone you trust who has bought something from you. Ask them for feedback on what their experience was like and how you can improve the sales process.

Date to review:

Chapter 23

BRIGHTEN UP YOUR GAME

To build a new brand you have to be far enough away from the biggest brand. Consider how Lowe's has managed to compete with Home Depot – their aim in many ways is to appeal to women. We used to think Lowe's was second place, maybe not.

Be proactive.

What does that mean exactly? It means do it before you're told. Do it before it becomes obvious it should've been done.

Always reinforce the value of your products to your customers: "That's a great choice, Ms. Jones."

Align yourself with your customers' needs, and then talk to them in *their* language (i.e., if you're in computers, most laypeople won't understand your lingo, so talk to them in a way that they can understand you).

Always give what you promise and more if it's possible. If you have promised a customer five items, and they get six, they're happy. If you've promised a customer five items and they get four, you're about to be in a position that's not enviable! I remember purchasing a shirt online that also came with a free accessory. I ended up buying two of the shirts, but still got only one of the accessories. I didn't complain, since it was free, but *still* I feel I should have received two accessories as that's what was advertised.

Plan. Anticipate what your customer's next move might be so you're ready for it.

Find out your industry's benchmark and whether you're providing that quality of service. If not, what'll it take?

In my seminars I often ask people whether they're offering any lifetime services to their customers, or sending thank-you notes or simply just following up after the sale. More often than not, they say no! When they find out these things are industry standards, their ideas change.

THE BENEFITS OF PROACTIVITY

Being proactive allows you to feel like you have some control over your life and your destiny – even if plans change quickly. I met a business acquaintance for breakfast the other day, and I noticed he was wearing a magnificent suit with a well-starched shirt. During breakfast, he spilled ketchup on his shirt. No matter, he said, he had another one hanging in the car!

Again, plans change quickly, so we might as well be prepared for the worst.

Being proactive consists of precisely that: being "pro" and "active." Planning things and getting them done builds self-esteem. Self-esteem comes from producing results that make a difference. Most of us are constantly in a state of reactivity. We may even be highly successful in our careers and family, but it's based on reactive thinking. In this mode of living we don't shape life but allow it to "happen" to us.

Think how much better it feels when you plan something and then make it happen. Compare it to what it feels like when someone else plans it for you and requires an action of you. Being proactive is being in charge, and it's being in charge of you. It might not always work in your favor but you have a better shot than if you leave it all up to chance.

So how do you become proactive? First, determine a goal for yourself. It may be in your relationships, your personal life or your business. It doesn't matter what it is, but pick something so you can be on your way.

Next, get the information you need that will help you accomplish the goal. If you want to be a better golfer, maybe you need some golf books and videos or a trip to a golf school. You'll need all the right information if you're intent on grabbing life by the horns. I know I always feel better if I have a list to work on in the morning—usually something I've prepared earlier that week or possibly the night before. It's much more difficult when I plan my day that same morning. I have less of an idea of how long each task will take or which ones are the most important. Then I make myself feel nervous because I feel like I'm wasting time putting the plan together.

Carefully review your steps. Do you need a script to make it work, or a checklist of dates and times? What about the size of your plan; is it too complicated? If it's complicated break the steps down so they're manageable.

Think about what might get in the way of your steps. If your goal is to lose 10 pounds in the next three months, you'll need to plan meals, what you want to eat and also where you're going to eat. I find it amusing when I conduct workshops with people who have goals to lose weight, and then see them constantly nibbling at the cookie table. They often say, "I didn't know there would be cookies! I just can't resist them." It makes sense though. Recovering alcoholics talk about staying away from places where alcohol is served because it's too tempting.

Develop a way to deal with problems before they become all you think about. Then decide what needs to happen to overcome the problem and how you are going to do it. If you're aiming for five more sales appointments this next week, how much more time do you need to spend on the phone to get them, or how many more networking events do you need to attend? Write down the different options available to you to move beyond each problem as it arises.

DEVELOPING A PROACTIVE NATURE

A great way to develop a proactive nature is to keep on top of the little things that make up your life. Get extra kitty litter; make sure there's a full tank of gas in your car; save a little extra money in your account each week so you don't run out. This is being proactive. You don't want little things to get in the way of your big things. I can't believe how often I hear people use traffic as an excuse as to why they're late to meetings. If they knew there was so much traffic at that hour of the morning, why didn't they get up earlier to avoid it?

How badly do you want to get things done? Do you guilt yourself into doing things? Do you allow irrelevant things to distract you from the bigger picture? "Don't let things that matter least get in the way of things that matter most," the old saying goes. Funny how the more clear we become on what's important to us, the more proactive we tend to become.

Find out what drives you.

Action steps

- Establish benchmarks to determine how proactive you and your staff are. Create time-based checklists for sales calls, follow-ups and customer feedback forms.
- Keep track of how you spend your day. Finalize each day's schedule the night before, and then evaluate how well you stuck to it at the end of the day.

Date to review:

Chapter 24

How Do You Know Who You've Lost?

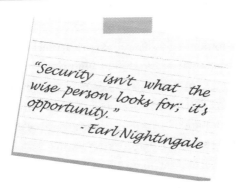

"Security isn't what the wise person looks for; it's opportunity."
- Earl Nightingale

Customer retention strategies should be one of the key focuses of any business. Consider the following statistics:

- The probability of selling to an existing customer is 60%-70%, while there's only a 5%-20% chance that you'll sell to a new prospect – and that's only after you've done all the work to *find* the new prospect. (Marketing Metrics)
- A 10% improvement in customer retention results in a 30% increase in the value of the company (Bain & Co.)
- A 5% increase in customer retention can increase business profits by 25%-125% (Gartner Group)

In other words, having your brand implanted firmly in a customer's mind is the greatest goal any business owner could ever strive for. With that in mind, how many customers have you lost this year? If you're like most companies, 10% - 40% of your customers have walked away and will never return. When you lose a customer, you lose more than just revenue. You have to go out and find new customers to replace the lost ones – and that can be costly and time-consuming.

Not knowing what customers you've lost is as important as knowing what customers you have. Maybe I buy from you because you are (a) close by, (b) I know you, or (c) I bought from you before. The thing is, most people don't spend time finding out why their customers buy. Many successful salespeople haven't even figured out why it's so important either.

When customers leave, they take vital pieces of information with them about why they left, and that is what we want to figure out.

I just returned an item to a rather high-end store. The store is part of a local museum so the items are unusual. I bought a watch with an interesting watch band – so interesting in fact that I realized that when it wears out or gets out of shape, there will be no way to replace it. So as unique it was, it would have a limited lifespan. I went back to the store and the woman there wasn't very customer-service oriented. In fact, it seemed she was working overtime to get me to wish I had never been in there. Statements like "Aren't you worrying about something that hasn't happened?" and "No one else complained" really *don't* provide for a good customer service experience.

Her comments brought up feelings of helplessness as well as anger. I realized that they were designed to intimidate or make me question whether I really should bring it back. I ended up getting my money back, but obviously left with an angry feeling about the salesperson and the store. If I were truly devious, I could spread rumors that the store's merchandise is suspect. But it's not true. The store is great; it just had what I consider to be an inexperienced salesperson. Had she been nicer I might have left with a good feeling and been willing to send people there.

This is feedback the store – particularly the owner – could use. How many customers have felt the same way? The customer's feelings and behaviors are important for a store to consider if they want to improve their customer service. An angry customer is probably not going to send customers your way.

To continue with the story, a strange thing later happened with this store. I received a call from the owner who said my name was on a memo pad on her desk, and she wasn't sure why she needed to call me. I said it might be about crediting back my credit card, and that I was glad she called so I might remember what card she credited and what date. She said she had no idea, and since she didn't keep her credit slips it wasn't easy for her to find out. From my perspective, all she needed to do was call the store and ask the staff to look it up, but she instead insisted I needed to go there to figure it out myself.

I couldn't believe she said that! As if that weren't enough, she then added that someone had come in and bought the watch a day later and said it was beautiful! Was that even relevant to the conversation?

I realized I'd had enough – I was angry! I opened up my credit card statement the other day and found a charge from this store for a gift I'd purchased earlier for my sister. I asked the card company to protest the charges. Why? Maybe it will help the store remember which credit card they charged for the watch.

The lesson in this: don't make the customer mad. It's one thing to not care if you lose a customer, but quite another to go out of your way to try to make them feel guilty. This can only hurt your business!

TAKE INVENTORY

Consider these points when evaluating the current state of your business.

- Who do you know for sure you've lost?
- Which transactions are not yet complete?
- Check the cancellations. Which customers were they and how much did you lose?
- Check which customers have come in, said they would be back, but haven't returned yet.

Your customers hold valuable information for you. Don't ask your salespeople why a customer may not have bought, because they'll just assume it's the prices. It *certainly* wasn't that the salesperson was agitated, confrontational, fidgety, trying to rush the customer or annoyed that the customer interrupted his T.V. time.

Remember, the customer is the main source of your information – not the salesperson. It's the customer's perception of what happened that is needed. Even if they're making stuff up, you still need their perspective because that's what's going to help you avoid future problems.

In graduate school I took a class in psychology and law. We read several books and articles supporting the theory that eyewitness testimony is the least accurate evidence available. In fact, the professor illustrated this with a little skit. In the middle of class someone ran in and grabbed the professor, wrestled him to the ground, took his wallet and then ran out the door – right before our astonished eyes! A student picked up the professor, dusted him off and asked if he was okay. He kept asking what people noticed about the assailant: the color of hair, color of skin, sex. There were as many ideas as there were students. At the end he explained what he had done and invited the "perp" into the class. Only one person had the assailant's profile correct.

So, get to the customer and then ask them directly what they think.

The next order of business is to figure out how to help them reveal what they think. Ask them what they think is important to the "thrival" of your store (that's a cheesy combo of "thrive" and "survival" – you may not want to use it). Also, tell them what is important to *you* about your store, and see if that's what's getting across. Is it a clean parking lot, smiling salespeople, clean showroom?

I did a survey for a distributor and asked who in the business makes the most difference to them. We listed everyone who had contact with the customer and I had to fight hard for the trucker's name to get on the list. It turned out the truck driver was seen as the most influential – so influential that we sent the salesperson out with the truck driver to find out what magic the truck driver had. It turned out he helped his customers unload products from the truck – which he didn't have to do – and was always in good humor. It had a tremendous effect on people.

FIGURE OUT WHAT YOUR CUSTOMERS ARE WORTH

Wouldn't it be great if one lost customer was just one lost customer? Unfortunately that's not how it works. Statistics tell us that an unhappy customer will tell many people while a happy customer will probably only tell one!

Another statistic tells us that it takes one wrong to counteract 10 rights. By losing a customer, you can be sure that this person will now go and talk with at least as many people as will listen, who will then speak with their friends and so on and so forth. This is what we call the ripple effect. One lost customer may not be the end of your business, but many of them could be. Financially, it's worth looking into why any customer is lost.

THE LOST CUSTOMER

What is a lost customer? It's someone who used to do business with you but doesn't anymore. It could be someone who was *close* to doing business with you but who isn't any more.

Not all customers go elsewhere for the same reasons.

Customers will tell you what they think is palatable to you as to why they left. The common complaint is that your price is too high. Retailers seem to like that explanation, to blame it on the salespeople and call it a day.

My experience is that customers lie when it comes to why they defected, and the "price is too high" objection means different things to different people.

Your price is too high may mean that the outside of your business looks like a warehouse. If I think warehouse prices are cheaper and I walk in and notice your store isn't a warehouse, I'll probably go elsewhere.

Considering the effects of one lost customer, it makes perfect sense to have someone contact them to discover the real reason. You want to hire someone who's not associated with the store and who has no vested interest in what the answers are. Find out if your perception matches the customer's perception of why they didn't buy. Is this a long-standing customer? Why would a long-standing customer find a reason to go elsewhere? How much revenue did you send your competitors? How many new "toys" has the competition sold to your lost customers? This information is bound to get everyone off their rears and in gear. Losing customers is one thing but paying your competitors a commission is another thing.

Is it possible to get this customer back? My experience from having conducted many studies is that salespeople give up and stop calling customers for any number of reasons, one of which is that it's not "nice" to bother people.

Remember, this is not a job for anyone associated with the store; you'll find yourself making excuses, telling the customer they misunderstood and everything you can think of to justify inappropriate behavior.

Many stores have salespeople call customers after the job is done, thinking that customers will tell the truth. The only way, again, you'll get this important information is from someone not connected to you who's not biased and doesn't care what you've done and has no reason to please you.

Find out, and then fix it.

This reminds me of a couple of lines from the movie, *The Big Night*. The movie is about two Italian brothers in the restaurant business. The chef wants people to eat what he thinks they should eat and wants to cook his way. The brother, who's the waiter, is just trying to make money. In one scene, a customer asks for rice and spaghetti on the same plate. The chef is outraged, saying that amount of starch together should be illegal! The waiter, meanwhile, is yelling at him to just make the dish!

Your goal is to give the customer what he wants. If you lose a customer, find out why and then aim to rectify it. Add a policy statement to your business so your customers – and employees – know you expect it not to happen again. Be careful of this one, though. Every time I see a sign that says, "We're not responsible for your coat being stolen from the coat rack," I know coats have already been stolen and the restaurant is simply giving the customers a heads up that they're not responsible, no matter what happens.

Are there awful customers? Of course! So it takes a lot of skill to deal with awful customers and to sell them.

If you lose a customer, think about different ways to win them back. First determine if it's possible, and then what it's going to take to do it.

Losing a customer is never fun, but it can be a learning experience. Remember, even nasty customers have money, and he who gets the money – while upholding their mission statement – wins.

Action steps

- Think of a time you've lost a customer. What would you have done differently?
- Look at how your staff relates to prospects. Do they aim to build a relationship? Do they go out of their way to assist them? How can you do better at turning prospects into customers?

Date to review:

Chapter 25

KEEP IN TOUCH WITH YOUR CUSTOMERS

"Customer service is not a department, it's an attitude."

- Anonymous

Is there such a thing as too much contact with customers?

The National Association of Sales Professionals says that 2% of sales are made on the first contact, 3% of sales on the second contact, 5% of sales on the third contact, 10% of sales are made on the fourth contact, and 80% are made on the fifth through twelfth contact! On average, it takes seven to twelve follow-ups for a person to buy from you, so you *must* keep in constant contact!

See if you can get a monthly newsletter together. E-mail this out to your customers to let them know what's going on with your store – whether it's a sale, a new item in or a promotional event. This keeps them in the loop, which will make them feel more compelled to go into your store again and again.

Send birthday cards and thank-you cards to customers.

If you're having any kind of sale, send a reminder via e-mail. Remember, the Web is a great way to keep tabs on your customers. Your Web site should have an opt-in e-mail field for addresses, which will then send your customers any and all updates you wish to send out. It's an inexpensive – or free – way to send notices.

Don't spam customers or pester them with cold calls – this is not a good way to keep in touch!

Just as auto oil-change shops keep tabs on their customers' cars, you should keep records on your customers and anticipate their needs. Keep a simple booklet of when you'll be getting new products or services, and compare them to the spending habits and likes of your customers. If you think they'd like to know about something, send them a card.

If you've had a customer who's been with you for years, you certainly should know their likes and dislikes by now. If a new product comes into your store that you believe would be of interest to them, give them a call just to let them know you were thinking of them when the product came in, and you'd love to have them stop by to see what is new.

This indicates to them that not only have you paid attention to them in detail, but that you care about them as well.

Sometimes people forget things. I know I do! If you have a doctor's appointment, most of the time you'll get a reminder call or note a few days ahead of time. Do this with your customers. If they've left something with you to be fixed, call them to let them know that it's ready to be picked up. After they've picked up their item from you, give them a call within two weeks to see how everything's holding up, and if there's anything else you can do for them.

I recently bought a used car. Now, everyone knows what one has to go through sometimes to get a car one really wants. So, after spending what seemed like eons with my new friend the car salesman, and thanking him profusely for getting me on the road in my fabulous car, I felt kind of sad having to say goodbye. Not as sad as when I saw how much my car payment was, of course, but sad nonetheless.

After a couple of weeks driving my car I noticed that the "check engine" light had come on. Naturally, I was terrified that I had just bought a lemon. But that couldn't possibly happen, right? Not after all the time I spent with this lovely man who was so genuinely excited to see me get what I wanted! Day after each crazy day, I kept meaning to call the place where I bought my car, but I kept finding new excuses to put it off.

I came home one night and there was a message from this man who sold me my car, who was calling to make sure I was still as happy with the car as I was the day I drove off the lot with it. Well, did I have a word or two ready for him! I called him back and he was helpful from the get-go. He told me to bring my car right in and they'd fix the problem immediately, free of charge.

Thankfully it ended up being something really small, and my car has since been fine. I found it so meaningful that he had checked up on me, I ended up sending *him* a thank-you card!

A month or so passed after having my "dummy light" – as they called it – fixed, and I came home to another phone call from my lovely car salesman. He was calling, once again, to check that everything was okay. I called him back with a smile on my face, and thanked him for taking the time out of his day to call me. Everything was great, and I knew that if it weren't, I could call on him and he'd help. He told me how nice it was doing business with me, and that if, in the future, I or anyone I knew was in the market for a new car, he would love to be of assistance.

I know in the back of my mind that this was all a way to get me to go back there, and nowhere else, and to get my friends and family to go there. And you know what? It worked. He did make me feel special and taken care of. Calling to check up on me and my car was the icing on the cake.

Action steps

- What customer information collection system do you have in place?
- Consider how you can up-sell or offer discounts to move more products or services.

Date to review:

Chapter 26

GIVE CUSTOMERS INFORMATION THEY NEED

"Here is a simple but powerful rule: always give people more than what they expect to get."

- Nelson Boswell

Customers know what they want, but do they know what they need? It is up to you to figure that out by continuing to ask them questions.

Don't assume the customer knows anything that you know about your product. Explain to them what they are buying, and why it is a good investment. They need to know what they are getting and why. This also helps for when they want to explain it to their friends—and then tell them where they got it!

I went to a Starbucks at yet another airport and asked the barista if she had tried the orange cocoa latte. She wrinkled up her nose as if I had asked, "How's the rat poison?" She said, "I don't drink coffee much; and most of this is too sweet anyway." For fun I asked her, "Did they ask you if you liked coffee when they hired you?" She replied, "To work here you don't have to like the coffee. Besides, I find it too expensive."

This didn't seem like the usual Starbucks barista. After trying my $3.60 drink I began to rethink my morning. Does a customer really care about what I think when it comes to their buying habits? Is it my business whether a customer likes one of my products over another?

Employees – the internal customers – need to support their business, the products and the customers. That doesn't mean they can't have their own likes and dislikes. I loved hearing her mind, and I really liked her take on things – it got me thinking. At the same time, did she really want to continue working at a place where she didn't really believe or support the products and services? She was right though. The orange cocoa latte was a little sweet.

Action steps

- Set up periodic meetings so your staff can give you and the business an appraisal. That is, where they can share anything and everything on their minds.

Date to review:

Chapter 27

ARE YOU TURNING OFF CUSTOMERS
WITHOUT EVEN KNOWING IT?

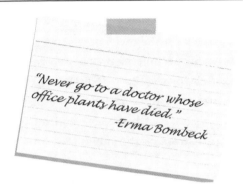

"Never go to a doctor whose office plants have died."
-Erma Bombeck

What happens to your business if you continually turn off customers?

You won't have a business for very long, that's what.

Treat all customers as important and let them know they're valued. If a customer needs answers, get them the answer quickly. If you don't know the answer but say you'll find out, be sure to find out quickly. I was in a big chain store once trying to find an answer to my question about replacing a ceiling light. I met four people on my way to the lighting department who said, "I don't know but I'll find out." By the time I got to the lighting department, I had a feeling the place was filled with people who didn't know anything!

Develop a customer-first culture by making customers feel good and making sure you give a good first impression. Smile. Stop to talk to them. Salespeople often avoid customers who are already "spoken for" by another salesperson, but the truth is, the customers in the store are everyone's customer. They keep the business going.

You can be pretty sure that if a customer needs to use your restroom, and it's not spotless, they'll be turned off. This is a sign of how clean the rest of your store is. For those of you who do work in your customers' homes, the state of your store might tell me that's how you're going to leave my home when you've finished working!

If you work in retail, make sure to clean out the dressing rooms after each use. I laugh when I go to Macy's. The clothes hang so neatly on the racks, but when I go into the dressing room I find tons of clothes lying on the floor and over the benches. Now, even when I see clothes hanging nicely on the racks at Macy's, I can't help but think they've been strewn all around the dressing room!

Speaking of clean, I've heard airlines recommend that their customers *not* reach into the middle seat pocket, since that's often where diapers, garbage, barf bags, etc., end up. I always wondered why flight attendants wore plastic gloves to clean – now I know!

MAKE SHOPPING AN EXPERIENCE

Shopping should be fun. When you make your store fun your customers will find it easier to shop. Put shopping carts and baskets around the store so people will be able to buy more. It *isn't* fun carrying an armload of items around the store. You can be sure if you see a customer with her hands full, she's probably not that happy with you. I've always wondered why supermarkets don't put more baskets and carts around the interior of their store, since people can easily get overwhelmed with what they pick up. I know I limit what I pick up because I know I have to carry it to the front.

Look at how your signage impacts your customers as well. We live in a world where computers and printers are things of every day use. It's easy to get signs printed. Hand-printed signs posted inside or outside your store can be a turn-off. To many people, this may say that you either don't care to take the time to make something nicer on a computer, or you don't have the money to do so. If you don't have the money to do so, then what kinds of products must you be selling?

I remember seeing a brightly-lit marquee on top of a building that spelled "Carpet Store," except the C had gone out so it read "arpet

Store." It was like that for three months. I finally stopped in to ask what an "arpet" was. Everyone laughed and wondered why I didn't know it meant *Carpet*. I was really only trying to make a point!

As of last week, the C was still missing.

AROMAS

It's always nice to walk into a store and have a beautiful scent hit you instead of floor disinfectant. I can't believe how many restaurants I've been in where staff will start washing the floors with Clorox while I eat. It's actually not a problem for me – it brings back memories of when my aunt used to clean up during Thanksgiving dinner. Somewhere between the entrée and the dessert, she would sweep the floor and then clean with Pine Sol disinfectant. It seemed annoying at the time, but to this day Pine Sol makes my mouth water. Most customers, however, probably don't have the same fond memories of Clorox or Pine Sol as I do.

Try not to give customers a headache. A great scented candle or potpourri might be grand, but don't overpower the customers with a scent *you* love, because they may just think it's awful. If you must eat lunch in your store, be sure to bring in something that is completely "smell proof." Nothing with onions or tons of garlic where people feel like they've just walked into a food store (unless they have!). I was on the plane the other day polishing a nail and the flight attendant came over and told me it wasn't acceptable. I told her I was just trying to combat the odor of fried onions and peppers to the right of me. She didn't think it was funny. I didn't mean it to be funny!

Granted, what turns one person off may actually please another.

I used to know a retailer in Yonkers, NY, who would cook Italian on Fridays. He'd fry tons of garlic, open the doors and put a big fan in the doorway to blow the aroma out the door. Women would stop in just to ask for recipes. That's one way to get them in the store! If your store is in an Italian neighborhood, garlic might be a good strategy.

MUSIC

A really good way to turn off a customer is to have loud, obnoxious music playing in the background, unless that's what your customers demand. The latest trend in music is to have tunes that your customers can sing to. This means providing a variety of music – often Top 40 – in order to appeal to a variety of customers.

I was in Spencer Gifts with an 80-year-old friend who was shopping for a black light for a 14-year-old. The music was earth shattering. My friend told me that the music would drive her out of the store — didn't they realize? I told her, frankly, they probably didn't want 80-year-olds anyway as it was bad for business!

On the flipside of loud music, silence is awkward for both customers and salespeople. The salespeople start making up things to say and customers look for places to hide so they can whisper to their friends.

The atmosphere should energize your customers, unless you're selling caskets. I spoke with someone who sold caskets and he said you know you've got the customer when they start to cry. I wondered if he played sad music in the store to help get them to cry faster.

In any event, know the demographics for your customers and what they respond to. What type of music do they like and what stores play their kind of music? Remember, don't judge a book by its cover; just because the customer looks a little older doesn't mean they didn't go to Woodstock!

LIGHTING

Good lighting makes a lot of difference. Have different types of lighting in your store. Natural lighting is always safe. Fluorescents, on the other hand, can really change the colors. My friend bought a sweater in Marshalls once and called me from the store to tell me it was the "perfect peach color." When she got home she called to tell me someone must have switched the colors – it was now bright pink!

Customers want to see what they're looking at. If you've got bulbs that are burned out, change them as soon as you see them. It reflects on you and how well you take care of your store. If your customer happens to be over 40, it might be a good idea to carry "cheater" glasses – once known as reading glasses – which improve optical clarity and don't require a prescription.

Also keep an eye out for stains in the ceiling, damaged tiles or stains on the floor. Fix it or cover it up. Become a master at repairs or have someone on call who can fix it. Ignoring these things tells people you're lazy, can't see or just plain don't care. Which one works for you? Speaking of stains, if you have to move things around at your job, keep an extra shirt around in case you need to change.

SINCERITY

Be sincere with your customers. Women know when they look good and when they don't – if I'm having a bad day we all know it's so. Watch out if you're being fake or "trying too hard." Both of these take away from your credibility and build distrust. Remember, you're always going for trust.

Take time to look at the customers and how they dress. What statement are they trying to make? Can you compliment them and feel good about it? Trying to *be* like your customers is part of building rapport – but don't get caught up in a lie.

A salesman confided to me once a whopper of a lie he told. A pregnant customer had come into his store. She said she was having twins in three months and he replied that so was his wife. Truth was, he wasn't married, nor was his girlfriend even pregnant. Some months later he bumped into her in a Kmart and she asked if his wife had had the twins and how were they? He had a tough time keeping up the façade of the lie while his girlfriend stood right by, no doubt wondering what was going on. I wonder how much longer his girlfriend stayed with him.

People value honesty and often know when they're being patronized. If a customer tries on a pair of sunglasses and the customer asks you what you think, suggest that she try on a couple of pairs so you have something to compare. Some people actually look good in lots of things; the question really is, what do they like *best*?

I was in a store and as I came out with a sweater on, the salesperson immediately complimented me on how it looked. I went back into the dressing room and a customer there stuck her head around the door and said, "It's too big for you." Frankly, I liked it and bought it – but I was forced to think about it first.

Who knows what people want? Only they do. Give them choices so they can compare and make their own decisions. You don't want to have "the only opinion." And you also never want to criticize a customer. Saying they look "terrible" in something – unless they love you and your taste – will guarantee they won't be back. Instead, offer them a few options. This might still suggest "terrible" but at least it's in a nicer way. The customer knows your job is to sell them, but they're hoping you're their friend as well and will sell them what's right for them.

There's a saleswomen I know who works in the fitting room of a popular chain store. She always passes comments on people's clothing – but she does it in a way that makes you want to listen. She'll say things like, "blue brightens up your complexion," "brown is too subtle for you," "black makes you look elegant." From those comments customers can decide whether they want to look bright or elegant. They also realize you're there to sell them something that is right for them, rather than for you.

Don't judge customers by their appearance. This cannot be said enough. If a customer walks in with diamonds up to her elbows, and she is then followed by a customer with a scraggly haircut and ripped pants, do *not* assume you know which one will be the bigger spender.

Of course, everyone has a "farmer in the overalls with $5,000 cash in his pockets" story. Here's another one:

My friend told me about his experience selling RV's. On his first day on the job, the first customers who came to him were scraggly and had dirty nails. The woman smelled of too much cheap perfume. My friend took this all in and decided to show them some lower-end items on the lot. The customers asked, "Do you have anything better?"

My friend showed them the next lowest-end items on the lot. They again asked, "Do you have anything better?'

Bottom line, they left a $25,000 deposit on a $65,000 RV. Why did they look so bad? Simply put, they owned a huge llama farm and were hands-on owners. They'd actually just come from helping a llama give birth, which explained their disheveled appearance.

The longer you're in customer service, the more experience you'll have with this. By paying more attention to the diamond-clad lady, you may have just turned down your biggest sale of the year – and not only that sale, but any other sale that the neglected customer would have referred your way.

If possible, have at least two phone lines in your store, even if your store is small. There is nothing more frustrating than trying to get through to someone and getting a busy signal for an hour. Now you've turned a customer off before they've even entered the store!

If a line is forming at your check-out stand, get another colleague to come up and help you. No one wants to wait in line. Remember, we live in an impatient world!

Most patrons know what time your store is closing. Turning on the vacuum cleaner while they're still there is not going to make them do anything but get angry and feel no need to come back to your store. If it seems a particular person is just not leaving in time, remind them that your store is closing and you want to make sure they've got everything before you close.

Don't forget that it takes only one bad experience to wipe away ten good ones.

Action steps

- Look at anything in your store that might be a potential turnoff to customers.
- Find out what competing businesses do to create ambience in their stores. Does it work? Why or why not?

Date to review:

Chapter 28

DEVELOP A CUSTOMER PROFILE

"Customer service is awareness of needs, problems, fears and aspirations."

- Anonymous

A big problem shared by many businesses is that they really don't know their customers.

Knowing your customer, why they buy from you and what they like about you will help you develop a customer profile. Once you have this profile you can look for more customers that fit the profile and then determine the best ways to attract these customers.

These days, however, it's very hard to peg a customer. There was once a time when you could tell wealthy customers by how they dressed and conducted themselves. Same with the poor customer.

These days, people can dress well and have no money, or dress poorly and have plenty of money. It doesn't matter what "side of town" you live on either. One of my doctor friends lives in what could be considered the bad side of town. He lives there because he was able to buy a huge, magnificent house for next to nothing. He has bars on the windows and tries not to park his car in the neighborhood on weekends. He probably doesn't get any direct mail from high-end stores, even though he's got a high-end checkbook!

To develop a profile of your customers, ask yourself the following questions and revisit them every week:

- What's common among my customers who spend money? Is it their age? Profession? Are they all soccer moms?
- What do my customers like about our salespeople and our showroom?
- What keeps my customers coming back?
- How well do we handle complaints?
- Do we keep track of customers' spending habits?
- What do our customers like or dislike that we have to offer them?
- If customers have a complaint, how do they feel about the way our team handles it?
- Are they repeat customers? If so, what keeps them coming back?

Ask them!

Once you've developed a sense of what your customers want, decide how you can give it to them. What changes do you have to make to satisfy your customers?

Keep track of customer purchases. To keep your store in your customers' minds, send them coupons that they can redeem for merchandise. If your ticket is quite large and customers only buy your product infrequently, consider another approach. How about a coupon for customers who bring in friends? They can redeem it for a nice bottle of wine.

Thank-you notes are always excellent to send to customers.

Send out notices to previous customers about upcoming sales events. Statistics tell us that the best source of business is the customer who has just made a purchase.

Include those who've been in your store but haven't yet made a purchase. Customers who haven't made a purchase are like gold that hasn't been discovered – sometimes you just have to dig further to find it. Not all customers are the "low hanging fruit" we all crave.

If you've found that your customer base is, say, in their teens to early 20s, promote items that will keep them coming back. Have a sale just for students (with valid student IDs). Offer monthly drawings to local spas or tanning salons, where the price is a dollar per ticket. Something affordable for today's students. The point is, know your target audience and try and reel them in with things that appeal specifically to them. If your target is older women, have things in the store that will appeal to them.

There are many things you can bring in that could widen your customer base, but before you do that, you want to be sure that you can keep the ones you have. In order to do so, putting out a little extra money for things that will speak to them might be worth it. It's going that extra mile, paying attention and listening to *their* needs and wants. This is what will make your store successful.

If you don't have a customer list, start one today. Even those who haven't bought anything yet should be on it. Your excitement about products and your expertise can turn curiosity seekers into buyers.

Action steps

- Start a customer profile list. Research ways to attract more customers through your regular print ads but also through online channels.

Date to review:

Chapter 29

PROMISE ONLY WHAT YOU CAN DELIVER

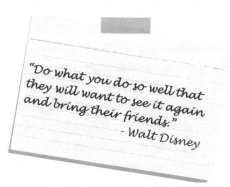

"Do what you do so well that they will want to see it again and bring their friends."
- Walt Disney

I still don't understand the old saying "Under promise and over deliver." It tells me that it's good to offer to do less than the minimum and then – *surprise* – do more. Well, the minimum isn't good enough anymore, since everyone wants more and more.

There's a book from Lowes Hotels called *Chocolates On the Pillow Aren't Enough*, which explains how putting one chocolate on a pillow nowadays is antiquated, since customers now expect the entire box!

Should you promise something you can't deliver? Well, that would be called "over promise and never deliver." It won't build good feelings or help your reputation.

How often do you hear the saying "It'll just be a minute!"? I hear it often at department stores as well as at airline ticket counters. I have never seen anything done in a minute though. There's nothing wrong with having customers wait a minute or a few minutes – and most will of course be patient. But at least be honest with how long it's going to take. If it's going to take 10 minutes, don't say "It'll only take a moment." People want to be able to manage their time and expectations. The clearer you can be with them, the better. When you obfuscate (love that word) or talk around an issue, it'll only foster resentment.

A friend of mine who wanted her living room painted received an estimate and time table over the phone that, she later realized, was simply too good to be true. Why don't people listen to their gut feelings? The painter came in, took a look at the walls and then said he'd have to do some extra work by sanding down the walls. The job would be done in three days. I couldn't imagine how in the world it would take three days just to paint one room, but hey, who knows? The price even seemed ridiculously low. So low, in fact, that my friend felt like she was stealing from the painter. The days came and went and the house just seemed to get worse and worse. She ended up firing the painter. Of course, she had a bigger mess than when she started since she now had to pay to get the mess fixed!

Be realistic in how you present your services or products to your customer. If you can't do the job, don't say you can.

There are times when it's not a bad idea to fudge the details a little bit, if it'll get a good response from your customer. If, for example, they know you're getting in a new product and are looking forward to seeing it, let them know when it will be in, but add a couple days to your expected "real" delivery time. When the product comes in early, give the customer a call. They'll not only be thrilled that it's in so quickly, but be impressed with how well your company must work to get things done so fast! This also allows for some leeway in the event something does actually happen while it's being shipped.

When you give the customer something they didn't expect, they remember it. Volley for the Cure is a non-profit organization designed to raise money and awareness for breast cancer through volleyball. The organization supplies high schools throughout Ohio with pink volleyballs and hosts charity matches between teams, with all funds raised going towards the organization.

A woman named Barb McGrath and her daughter Sara started it to honor two friends suffering from breast cancer. "Since we can't take chemo for them we did this instead," Barb said in USA Today. Their goal is to introduce the volleyballs in all of the state's high schools.

The founders of this organization are clearly experts at customer service. They raised awareness for a noble cause (cancer), introduced it to a highly influential demographic (teenage girls) using a popular sport (volleyball) and developed a brand exclusive to Ohio and possibly beyond. Who can forget pink volleyballs and the bleachers filled with pink t-shirts?

Customer service is giving the customer more than they expect — and then giving them more! But it's not about under promising.

Strive to make a difference and be the difference

My friend told me she buys Clinique cosmetics. The other day she received in the mail a bunch of small samples of cream and eye make-up remover from her favorite sales girl. The note said, "I know you travel and I have these 'bite size' samples that would be great to carry on. Thanks for being my customer!"

Smart huh?

Action steps

- Some of the most successful companies started out by modeling themselves after other companies. Who is your role model as a company or business leader? What can you do differently to be more like them?

Date to review:

Chapter 30

THE GOOD, THE BAD, AND THE UGLY
CUSTOMER

"Your most unhappy customers are your greatest source of learning."

- Bill Gates

"The customer is always right" is simply a phrase used to help businesses remember that their customers are what keep their businesses running.

The obvious fact is: the customer is not always right. But you can't just come out and say that – especially to the customer! If you've been in business for a while, you've probably noticed three customer types: the good, the bad and what I'm going to call "the ugly." A good customer is someone who adds profit to your business. A bad customer is someone who takes away from your business. The ugly customer is someone who adds to your bottom line, but who takes you through the grinder in the process. You *like* having them for their business, and you would prefer *not* to lose them. At the same time, they are difficult to deal with and sometimes you wish they wouldn't frequent your business.

So how do you sensitively deal with the "ugly" customer? First, you must think "win–win" rather than "win-lose." If you go into any situation thinking "win-lose," your aim is simply to make the customer wrong – and you'll end up losing him.

When dealing with a sensitive situation, ask yourself these questions to determine whether the fight is worth it. Be honest with yourself.

- Is this a customer you want to continue doing business with? Is the hassle of dealing with him worth the money he's paying for your product or service?
- Is this a problem that can be easily solved, or has it escalated out of control?
- Will you be able to keep a level head while dealing with a possibly irate customer or will you make it worse?
- Is this a customer who has had numerous complaints or returns in the past?
- What do you have to lose by giving in to his demands? Is it money, loss of face, or is there an important business policy at stake? It's important to know what it is you're going for, and what you're giving up if you attain it.

If you take these things into consideration, you'll navigate through a conflict with greater ease. In business, we will always come across unreasonable people. The key to dealing with them is to take a step back, remember that we are in business, and do what it takes to keep people happy without selling the farm.

This is not something easily done, and sometimes it's downright impossible – but sometimes the impossible is where you learn.

If you happen to be dealing with a long-time customer, someone you want to keep, there are steps you may want to take to show that you're going the extra mile for them – within reason, as always.

When I worked at the high-end clothing store in Washington, DC we frequently sold evening gowns. Often, customers would purchase them on Friday and then return them on Monday – occasionally with lipstick marks on them. We always took them back though. The owner said it was good for business and they were good customers. Well, he owned the store and I didn't. Years later he went out of business.

don't know if it was the gowns or what, but I imagine it'd sure be hard to sell gowns with lipstick on them!

When dealing with customers, make sure you're clear about what the problem is. Listen, take mental notes and ask questions to clarify so you understand what the exact issue is. A lot of times, customers *themselves* won't know what the actual problem is – they've simply been simmering all day about something that has nothing to do with you. Repeat the problem back to the customer using *their words*. Don't come out with an interpretation of what they've said. This will only anger the customer further. Make sure you know the exact problem they're having, and if you are unsure, ask them politely to explain it to you again.

Let them know, nicely, that you have a store policy, and that while you understand their frustration, your policy is there to protect both the store and the customers. Before you say this you had better believe it and know what it means. Your policy is there to provide guidelines on how to proceed in such cases.

On the flip-side, while your policy is there to act as a guideline, don't refer to it as absolute law. Your policy doesn't explain everything and, in the end, nobody really cares about policy anyway! If you can't give your customers their money back, you might be able to offer something else – perhaps a one-time compromise of store credit.

If you can't do anything to help the customer, don't say you can.

Make sure this customer knows that you value them and their loyalty to your store, and you do want to make this right.

Never tell your customer outright that they are wrong; tell them that it's important that you uphold the policy and that you want to find a way to help them.

Remember the customer who had his pants lost at the dry cleaners? He happened to be a very well-known judge and needed those pants for a special occasion. Well, the dry cleaner had a sign on the wall that said: "Customer satisfaction guaranteed." The problem was, absolutely nothing could satisfy this customer other than taking the dry cleaners to the cleaners! Naturally, the dry cleaning business wasn't interested in taking part in its own demise. So, be careful with those "Customer satisfaction guaranteed" signs. Some people will interpret them literally.

BITING THE BULLET

If this is a valued customer whom you truly want to see back again in your store, just bite the bullet and give them their money back. Tell them, however, that you're doing it on this occasion because you value their business. The customer will be happy that they've gotten their way, but it will also keep them coming back. This doesn't mean that the customer won't still be a problem. This is certainly not what you want to do for every customer who has a complaint, but you may have to make an exception.

If you're dealing with a customer who has no previous history with you or someone who is creating a scene, (and you've already gone through the above steps), you'll just need to stand your ground and inform them there is no refund. Be polite but firm. You may need to ask them to leave the store. Again, do so politely but firmly.

When you're dealing with difficult customers, be careful about being addicted to being right. Deal with what is and not what has happened in the past or what might happen in the future. No matter how it sounds, everyone should benefit.

Other customers will value how you treat customers – even ones that are terrible – and how you protect your employees. This may sound harsh, but think of what it's doing to the customers who are witnessing what's going on. When the debacle is over, apologize to the people who've just had to watch this embarrassing scene, and simply move on and cut your losses.

I witnessed an irate customer calling a clerk names because of a mistake the *customer* had made. The clerk refused to back down, matched the pitch of the customer's voice but never the anger. The customer kept trying to bait the clerk but he refused to go for it and held his ground. The customer stormed out the door and was back in five minutes after he had calmed down.

If you get caught up in an argument, excuse yourself from the conflict. Get someone else to takeover. Believe it or not, it usually takes more guts to move on than to go in and pick a fight.

Action steps

- Review your store policy and make sure it's up to date.
- Ask for feedback – or even take a personality assessment test – to find out where you could improve when dealing with other people

Date to review:

Chapter 31

BONDING WITH YOUR CUSTOMERS

"Trust is built from shared experiences over time—experiences that tell us when someone has our best interests at heart. We give people our trust today and tomorrow because they have been trustworthy in the past."
- Michael Berg

The more you give to your customers, the likelier it is they'll stick with you. One way to achieve this is to allow them to test drive your products.

If you walk into Bath and Body Works, you'll notice that they have samples of every scent available for you to try. What a wonderful way for us, as consumers, to see if we actually *like* a product before we buy it.

Use your product so you know how it works. The salespeople in the jewelry department of Macy's wear the jewelry – lots of it. Did you ever notice that salesmen at car dealerships change their cars every month or so? How would you know the inner workings of your products if you didn't try them?

If you have a showroom, install your products in it. However they're intended to be used, use them. Walk on them, sit on them, wear them, drive them, clean them, scratch them. Heck, invite the dog!

Update your showroom products frequently. Get rid of "old" or "stale" stuff if you want to attract a better customer. Old stuff loses its value quickly. Old colors, outdated patterns or products just make you look out of style. Once you look outdated, customers will start asking for discounts.

If it's reasonable to let your customers try your products out in their home, let them.

VIRTUAL EXPERIENCE

Get people enrolled in your product or service before they've seen it. Brag about the glowing reviews on your products. How about using video blogs from customers who show how much they enjoy it? Nothing beats an excited and credible customer who loves you and your products.

If you're installing your product in the customer's house, take a photo of it and add it to your Web site. Be sure to be complimentary about the customer's home and their good taste.

Build a photo album of completed interiors. Experience shows us that some people like complete outfits when they buy clothing, while others will only buy something that goes with what they already own. If you don't have lots of photos, simply cut some out of magazines for customers to see. Show them what their house *could* look like.

Pottery Barn's catalogs show not only the products that they have for sale, but how they're being used in the homes of real-life customers. You can go to Pottery Barn's Web site to take a virtual tour of these homes.

Action steps

- Research the bigger retail stores and see how they're marketing their products and using experiential marketing to help educate their customers.

Date to review:

PART III

STAY ON TOP OF TRENDS

Chapter 32

CREATE A CAPTIVATING ONLINE PRESENCE

"Social media is not a fad. Nor is it something that will pass you or your company by. Gradually, social media will impact almost every role, at every kind of company, in all parts of the world."

- Forrester Research

Ten years ago the Web was a mystery to me. The first time someone mentioned the term, I twisted my head around to see where it was hanging in proximity to me. I had no idea what they were talking about. It's amazing to me how big the Web has become in such a short amount of time. In fact, it has become a lifeline for many businesses that want to succeed.

ABOUT THE INTERNET

Published annually, the Digital Future Report from the University of Southern California studies the use of online technology in the U.S. and 25 other nations. The study reveals that as of last year:

- 77.6% of Americans age 12 and older go online.
- 89.8% of American Web users have e-mail, and these users spend an average of 14 hours online per week.
- 49.2% of American users make online purchases.

I read a post on a blog the other day about what it meant to be on the Web. It occurred to me, quite suddenly I might add, that customer service has evolved into something beyond the face-to-face interactions between a couple of human beings.

In fact, the face-to-face interaction may even be obsolete.

With the Web the way it is now, we no longer need to be in the store with the salesperson; we simply rely on what our peers and others say about it.

Blogs, Facebook, YouTube, Twitter, etc., have replaced the traditional salesperson educating you in-store, in-person on what to buy and why. Just think about it. The telephone is no longer the main means of communication these days – and I include speaking via cell phone as well. You can text, e-mail, Skype and send pictures in just a couple of seconds.

Consider the rise of some of the top Web portals and social networking sites out there:

- **Facebook** is credited with helping millions of people connect with one another and build social communities online. Users can post photos, comment on others' sites, send video and share news.

- **Twitter** – A social networking site where users can create conversations, follow others' conversations and keep each other informed on what they're doing with short updates.

- **LinkedIn** - A business-oriented social networking list designed to help professionals make business connections.

- **Angie's List** – This is the Web world's equivalent of the Better Business Bureau. Angie's List allows customers to comment about businesses they've frequented. Some comments can make or break a business.

- **Blog** – A Web site that displays journal–style entries written by known and *especially* unknown authors. In 2007, Technorati tracked 74.3 million blogs and reported that 175,000 new blogs were being created every day. The most popular platforms are Blogger, TypePad and Wordpress.

- **YouTube** - As of 2006, YouTube solidified its lead as the premier distributor of video content on the Web, though services such as Vimeo are now running close behind.

- **Video E-mail/Blogging** – Technology that allows users to create quick videos to e-mail to others or post on their blog. Video is a popular way to improve one's site ranking on Google.

Frightening as it may be, understanding that there is another world out there that is influencing our customers is the first step in providing another arm of customer service.

YOUR ONLINE PRESENCE

In addition to providing basic information about your company, your products and your services, your Web site should be able to give the customer useful information that focuses on them rather than you.

These days, many businesses and entrepreneurs are opting to go with blogs as opposed to standalone Web sites. A blog, again, is an online journal, but it doesn't have to reveal anything a traditional journal does. Instead, it can be one way to communicate back and forth with your audience.

Blogs allow your audience to comment on your products, services, thoughts – anything. The more dialogue you can create, the better, as it establishes you as an expert in your industry. Consider the following statistics from Digital Marketing World Expo 2009:

- 89% of companies in a recent survey say they think blogs will be more important in the next five years.
- 22 of the 100 most popular Web sites in the world are blogs.
- Over 57 million Americans read blogs.

- 51% of blog readers shop online.
- 1.7 million American adults list making money as one of the reasons they blog.

Your site can be a great way to establish trust with the customer. Most people these days are researching stores and products online first before trying them in the stores. With a Web site (and a blog), you have the opportunity to educate your prospect and establish trust. In fact, with a blog, you have the means of creating a dialogue with your customers. They can actually provide feedback and reviews of your goods. You, in turn, can write anything you want! It's your site!

If the store is 20 years old, write about how it's changed during the 20 years and what you've learned. Write things that promote curiosity and interest to the customer. Let the customers know what organizations you belong to and why they're important.

People are mobile and are communicating all over the world. How many love-lifes have sprung up as a result of the Web?

I am constantly amazed at how many people visit matchmaking sites like eharmony.com and match.com. A friend of mine once fell in cyberspace love with a woman from Russia. In fact, the Russian woman said she was spending $1,500 to come over here and visit him. Why would someone need to look so far for a date? Can you imagine how this story ended?

Eharmony.com says 90 couples get married every day as a result of making a connection through their site. Match.com says if you can't find someone special in the first six months, they'll give you six months free.

The lesson in all this – even if you don't have a matchmaking service – is that your Web site should provide customers with information that is not only valuable, but that can show an obvious return on investment. In retail, your aim is to show the *benefits* of your product and service. Specifically, how your customer will feel once they're in possession of it. Strive to make your content appeal to their emotions, get them excited and make them want to go to your store to get more of whatever you are selling. Good feelings and the promise of an opportunity to develop a good relationship with someone is what will get them in the door.

One of the best sales tools, moreover, is a good review. If your site features products and services, make sure to provide a forum for customers to review the product. These days, in order to save time, people are simply going to a site, looking for a product and then choosing one based on nothing other than what other people are saying about it. If you're able to get good reviews of your product, you'll have a leg up over your competition.

ENGAGE OR DISENGAGE?

Ask yourself, "Does our site engage or disengage the customer?" How much time do you spend evaluating the experience for the customer? Customer service starts way before you meet the customers or have any interaction with them face-to-face, so what are you doing to persuade the customer to want to step into your brick–and-mortar store?

In her book, *Building Your Competitive Advantage,* Jayne Smith talks about the importance of providing data for the customer to help them make distinctions between you and the next guy. Hyundai boasts their 100,000 mile warranty; the Cleveland Clinic talks about how many people survive heart operations at their hospital. Morbid, but effective!

A friend of mine was telling me what it was like to sit in a restaurant and have a bird's eye view of the kitchen while the food was being prepared. Sounds like a novel idea, doesn't it? It is, until you see the salad maker with no gloves on tossing the lettuce. *If you're going to let people look in the kitchen, know what's going on in the kitchen*!

"Conversation is happening all around us," says Phil Gomes of Edelman Worldwide, an advertising agency. What is your conversation? Does your online conversation stimulate, or are you using the "old pitch" model to bring the customer in? I would think that the average customer has seen it and heard it all and mere conversation just won't do it anymore. You need to offer substance.

I bought a car not long ago and spent a lot of time with the local Lexus dealer. In fact, I basically thought I had found the car that I liked and asked the salesperson to "do some tidying up on the car," which of course he did. Somewhere between the tidying up and two days later, I found a car I liked better while searching online, and bought it. While I didn't think my actions were out of bounds, I did feel the salesperson deserved an explanation. So I called him and explained what I had done and also to thank him for his help. He was actually delighted I'd called. He said it was rare that a customer would call and explain why she ended up not buying from him.

RESEARCH WHAT YOU LIKE

Are you constantly evaluating and monitoring your online presence? Are you going to sites and finding words out of order, sentences missing, or even worse, sending a note through the "contact us" form and getting a reply three weeks later?

Are you building an online community for your store? Virtual communities are raging out there. Think of how much easier it is to get information in that world as compared to this world? When worse comes to worse you can divorce your online spouse, move away and never be the worse for wear! An online community is not so different from the traditional model of the brick-and-mortar community. The same ideas, the same thoughts and the same building of relationships – it just doesn't have the physical store to huff and puff and be blown down! A blog, again, provides a forum where information can be exchanged and is a critical factor in your online presence.

Do you know what they're saying about you out there? Find out! Google your own store name and see what comes up. If there are blogs about you, read them!

I have a friend who's a marketing director for a ceramic tile manufacturer. One day, another friend told him about a blog where a few customers were badmouthing the company as a result of one bad customer service encounter.

My friend said his store has very little online experience, which told me that no one was responding or reaching out to the unhappy customers!

In the end, my friend turned the incident around by connecting with the bloggers and flying five of them into town for a tour of the company's plant. They ended up writing glowing reviews after that.

A blog allows you to express a personality that people can relate to. It makes you and your company real. Your customers can know what you and your business are up to and how sincere you are about customer satisfaction.

Our world is filled with many different ways to communicate – ways that many of us once could have never even imagined in our wildest dreams. But, it's here, and that means we need to get with the program. A lot of work? Maybe. However, in the end, it's destined to pay off.

PODCASTS AND VIDEO BLOGS

When you've got the hang of the latest in blogging techniques, take your online conversation to the next level with podcasts and a video blog. These tools allow you to be the radio DJ you always wanted to be or the T.V. personality you're harboring within you. These formats are booming—even presidential candidates are using them these days!

A video blog and podcast offer additional ways to get your message out there. Plus, with search engines providing higher rankings these days for sites that feature elements other than just text, a video campaign and regular podcast post will get your site more visibility.

These are brand new channels for your business that you can use for free – you just need to get started on them.

Oh, and about the woman from Russia who was planning to come visit my friend? At the last minute, she said she needed $900 to make the trip or the U.S. government wouldn't let her in. In other words: no money, no visit. My friend politely declined and just like that, the lovely girl from Russia was gone. I suggested my friend share his story with one of the daytime shows. Certainly there'd be someone out there who'd have sympathy for him and call him up for a date!

Action steps

- Take stock of your current online marketing efforts to see where you're at.
- Build a blog into your Web site.
- Create profiles on popular social networking sites and start talking to others about your industry.

Date to review:

Chapter 33

With Web Marketing, Content is King

"The fact is, everyone is in sales. Whatever area you work in, you do have clients and you do need to sell."
- Jay Abraham

Once you have your Web site, blog and social media profiles up and running (Facebook, LinkedIn, Twitter, etc.), it's time to weave them all together. It's very easy these days to link all of these sites to each other – what you write on your blog can automatically be posted to your social media sites. By the same token, what you update on your social media pages can link back to your blog. While it might seem redundant, there is a purpose to posting the same information on different sites.

For one, not everyone will see your Facebook page or blog, but they might be following your updates on Twitter. Same goes for the other sites. Therefore, the more updates you have in a variety of areas, the more likely your message will spread.

This is all irrelevant, though, if your content isn't interesting or doesn't provide value to the reader.

Remember, content will always be king. Make sure that your marketing campaign – both online and in print – *helps* your target audience (i.e., customer), so that they get something of value through their association with you. The moment you cease to be interesting to them is the moment they'll stop following you. Yes, it sounds like an ungrateful audience you're dealing with, but with all of these applications being free (or nearly free), all you really have to do is invest in quality content, educate yourself on the workings of social networking, and you might very well find your business's next big whale.

That will have made it all worthwhile, yes?

For a good book on how to tie all of your online marketing campaigns together, check out *The New Rules of Marketing and PR: How to Use News Releases, Blogs, Podcasting, Viral Marketing and Online Media to Reach Buyers Directly* by David Meerman Scott. It's well worth the investment.

Action steps

- Create a 1-month, 3-month, 6-month and 1-year online marketing plan.
- Research what some of the top businesses are doing to spread news of their products and services via the Web.

Date to review:

Chapter 34

SMART E-MAIL MARKETING STRATEGIES

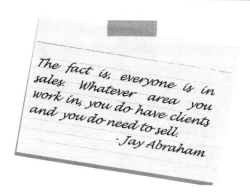

The fact is, everyone is in sales. Whatever area you work in, you do have clients and you do need to sell.
— Jay Abraham

I touched a bit on this before, but it's worth going into a little more. E-mail is one of your most powerful tools for communicating with people and building up a loyal clientele. While direct mail is still quite successful, it's also very expensive. With smaller budgets these days, e-mail campaigns and Web marketing have replaced much of what old-school print marketing did.

It's definitely worth your while investing in a bit of e-mail marketing know-how, and starting to collect client e-mails. For around $20 a month, you can take advantage of e-mail programs that will help keep your brand in front of customers, and keep your products in the forefront of their minds.

Any basic e-mail marketing software will give you the ability to:

- Manage a database of your customers
- Send e-mails to customers with periodic updates
- Send surveys and polls to customers requesting feedback
- Track how effective your e-mail campaigns are

The benefits of going with e-mail marketing software – rather than e-mailing from your own personal account – is that you can easily manage a list of customers' contact information, and you have a simple, powerful, inexpensive way of marketing to them. In addition, you'll be able to track how your campaigns are working. Many programs these days can figure out how many customers opened your e-mail and whether they clicked-through to the destination page – usually a landing page on your Web site.

A number of e-mail marketing tools also give you the ability to create online surveys and polls, making it easy for you to collect feedback from customers. This is an excellent benefit for business owners looking to conduct follow-up surveys after a sale.

Here are some of the most popular e-mail marketing tools available right now:

- aweber.com
- verticalresponse.com
- icontact.com
- constantcontact.com
- mailchimp.com

Most of these services charge a monthly fee, which depends on the number of e-mails you're sending out and the number of contacts in your list. Some providers, however, offer you the option of paying on-demand. So rather than paying monthly, you simply pay whenever you want to send a broadcast e-mail.

If you go with the monthly option, expect to pay $20-$30 a month for the first 1,000 e-mails you collect. If you're just starting out, it'll take you a while to get above 1,000 e-mails – unless you have a good following already! If that's the case, congrats! You're already way ahead of the curve.

BEST E-MAIL MARKETING PRACTICES

Remember, if you're conducting business or customer service online, you'll want to collect the e-mail addresses of any and all potential – and existing – customers. Your e-mail marketing software allows people to sign up for your services, giving you the power to send them e-mails whenever you have something to offer. The manager will automatically remove customers from your list whenever they opt-out, or unsubscribe. With this type of service, you're never at risk of being involved in spam issues. Customers receive e-mails at their own request.

It's important to take the utmost care when e-mailing your customers. Write professional copy and make sure that the e-mail content provides something of value to the customer. Are you announcing a discount? Offering coupons? Informing your audience of a sale?

Nothing will have customers unsubscribing faster than useless information.

Another important point is the timing of your e-mails. How many e-mails are too many? Some businesses e-mail weekly, some monthly, others – *gasp* – daily. This might work if you have incredible discounts and an eager fan base. However, for most businesses, less is best. E-mail whenever you have exciting news for the customer and something that will benefit them.

Lastly, try making your e-mail look nice. The above mentioned providers all offer the power of HTML e-mails, so you can design e-mails that people will not only enjoy reading, but enjoy looking at.

Action steps

- Sign up to receive e-mails from some of your favorite sites. Analyze how they're written and designed.
- Research how to write for the Web as opposed to writing for print
- Create a database of all existing customer e-mail addresses and add them to your new e-mail marketing service.

Date to review:

Chapter 35

KEEP MOVING FORWARD

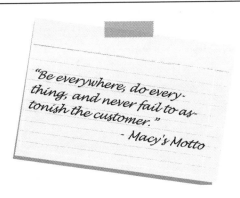

"Be everywhere, do everything, and never fail to astonish the customer."

— Macy's Motto

Well, dear reader, we've about come to the end of the book. I truly hope you've found some value within these pages, and some strategies that you can incorporate into your business that will help you become stronger, more effective, and more profitable.

A few final thoughts.

Strategies are not strategies unless the customer is involved. It's critical that business decisions you make are done with the customer in mind, and how they'll be affected.

Do your best to interact with your customers. No news is not good news when dealing with service issues. You want to know who's been happy, mad or sad today. If you don't know it's broken in life, you can't fix it.

Evaluate everything – from the way your store looks and smells to the color of the paint. Get it from the customer's view.

Form new alliances and partners – it's what will get you to the next generation of customers five to ten years down the road.

When it comes to feedback, don't accept anything that rates less than "great." Anything under 100% needs looking into. If your customer tells you she received 100% excellent customer service, see what you could have done to provide 110%.

There's always room for improvement no matter how good you are. Keep an eye out for new ideas and strive to keep learning. Like my father used to tell me, "Turn over every stone in the garden and something is bound to turn up."

Keep moving forward!

RECOMMENDED READING

Experience Economy: Work Is Theater & Every Business a Stage, Pine & Gilmore, Harvard Business School Press, 1999

Becoming A Person Of Influence: How To Positively Impact The Lives Of Others, John C. Maxwell, Jim Dorman, 1997

Chocolates On the Pillow Aren't Enough: Reinventing the Customer Experience, Jonathan M. Tisch, 2007

The Best Advice Ever Given, Steven D. Price, the Lyons Press, 2006

212: The Extra Degree, S.I. Parker, the Walk the Talk Company, 2005

It Takes a Prophet to Make a Profit, C. Britt Beemer, Simon & Schuster, 2001

Where Have All the Leaders Gone, Lee Iacocca, Scribner, 2007

Blue Ocean Strategy, W. Chan Kim, Harvard Business Review, 2005

The Origin of Brands, Al & Laura Ries, Collins, 2004

Creating Competitive Advantage, Jaynie L. Smith, Doubleday, 2006

Built from Scratch, Bernie Marcus and Arthur Blank, Homer TLC, 1999

Tales From Under the Rim: the Marketing of Horton's, Ron Bust, Goose Lane Editions, 2001

Made to Stick: Why Some Ideas Survive and Others Die, Chip Heath & Dan Heath, Random House, 2007

Treasure Hunt: Inside the Mind of the New Consumer, Michael J. Silverstein, Penguin Group, 2007

Blur: the Speed of Change in the Connected Economy, Stan Davis and Christopher Meyer, Ernst & Young Center for Business Innovation

Business @ the Speed of Thought, Bill Gates, Warner Books, 1999

The Power of the Purse, Fara Warner, Prentice Hall, 2004

On the Brin:, the Life and Leadership of Norman Brinker, Norman Brinker, Tapestry Press, 1999

Wear Clean Underwear: Business Wisdom from Mom, Rhonda Abrams, Villard Books, 1999

Teams that Click, Harvard Business School, Harvard University Press, 2004

The Satisfied Customer, Clases Fornell, Palgrave Macmillan, 2007

The Circle of Innovation, Tom Peters, Alfred A. Knopf, 1999

Living It Up: America's Love Affair with Luxury, James B. Twitchell, Simon & Schuster, 2002

The Tipping Point: How Little Things Can Make a Big Difference, Malcolm Gladwell, Little, Brown & Company, 2000

Pocketbook Power: How to Reach the Hearts and Minds of Today's Coveted Consumers – Women, Bernice Kanner, 2004

An American Success Story, Dave Longaberger, Harper, 2001

Time Traps: Proven Strategies for Swamped Professionals, Todd Duncan, Thomas Nelson, 2006

Mavericks at Work: Why the Most Original Minds in Business Win, William C. Taylor &P olly LaBarre. Harper, 2006

The New Rules of Marketing and PR: How to Use News Releases, Blogs, Podcasting, Viral Marketing and Online Media to Reach Buyers Directly, David Meerman Scott, Wiley, 2008

Buyology, Martin Lindstrom, Doubleday, 2008

Customers for Life: How to Turn That One-Time Buyer into a Lifetime Customer, Carl Sewell, Broadway Business, 2002 (revised)

ORDER FORM

For additional copies of this book:

Web: visit www.lisbethcalandrino.com
E-mail orders: lcalandrino@nycap.rr.com
Phone: 518 495-5380
Fax: 518 426-5812

Discounts available for books bought in bulk.

ABOUT THE AUTHOR

For more than 30 years, Lisbeth Calandrino has helped entrepreneurs, small businesses and corporations move to the next level in their industries. She has started and grown several successful businesses of her own, and now works full-time as a consultant and author.

As a public speaker, Lisbeth has spoken to thousands of people at seminars across the country, talking about the latest in business strategy and human potential. Her inspirational, humorous and high-energy approach to speaking has made her a highly sought-after business management coach. She is active in her community as a program planner and volunteer for Gilda's Club.

For updated tips and advice about how to boost your business and your bottom line, visit Lis's site at www.lisbethcalandrino.com. Join the growing community of professionals dedicated to providing *red hot customer service* at www.redhotcustomerservice.com/forum.